LIBERATION

Also by Anand Mehrotra

This Is That

Patanjali's Yoga Sutras

Padas 1 and 2

LIBERATION

An Interpretation of
Isha Upanishad

Anand Mehrotra

Sattva Publications

Cover illustration by Emma Abel

ISBN: 978-81-939882-3-7

Published by Sattva Publications
Rishikesh, India

For

Divine Mother

Introduction

Written at least 4000 years ago, the Upanishads use such incredible words, such wonderful sounds, and are filled with such diverse meanings, it is truly an extraordinary work. They are delivered with an elegant simplicity, such clarity, such precision of thought and yet they have such complex meaning it can only be the work of nature. The impulse of natural intelligence is expressed here with incredible complexity through elegant simplicity.

In his treatise on grammar, Patanjali says there are two kinds of Sanskrit scriptures: made by one and spoken by one. He makes that clear distinction between the two kinds of literary work in the Sanskrit teaching. Isn't that pure genius? 'Made by one' is used for stories, for myths, for legends and 'spoken by one' but not owned by the one who is speaking. For example, Hamlet was made by Shakespeare; he created that character but the Upanishads are not made by 'somebody'. They are cognitions that are shared.

The teachings of the Himalayan Yog-Vedantic tradition thrived in this geographical location; they were really developed and shared there. Yog being unity and yoga referring to the intention, the technology and the practice of it. And the intention of all these teachings is to experience them, to experience the progressive realization of unity from isolation. *Ved* means to know and vedanta means the ultimate knowledge, knowing that by which everything else is known. It is the ultimate knowledge because it is the knowledge of Self.

When one looks at the history of anything, one usually looks for written records. But before there is a written record, there has to be a thriving, complex, oral structure. Before you can write a complex book, you need to be part of a culture which is conversing within that knowledge already. There has to be a culture which has well-developed concepts and parameters before the written word. So one has to realize that the yogic teachings were fundamentally and predominantly an oral tradition with the written tradition being only an aid not a substitute. The written content, or nowadays the digital content, is not a replacement for the live, spoken tradition. Looking at the historical records from the yogic perspective, the Vedas are divided into four fundamental categories: Rig Veda, Sama Veda, Yajur Veda, which is further classified into two aspects, Shukla Yajur Veda and Krsna Yajur Veda, and Atharva Veda, in which the science of Ayurveda is located. Certain techniques and the word 'yoga' already start to be mentioned in Rig Veda.

All the Vedas, all teachings within the Sanskrit yogic tradition, are intentionally poetic in their nature. They are classified as shrutis meaning that they are heard. These are what the rishis, the yogis, the seers, heard when they got into a transcendent consciousness state. They are not creating this stuff and writing it down. This is a channelling. In the Vedic tradition, the texts are often anonymous, anonymous as in there is no singular author.

With the exception of a very few, there are no named authors of the Upanishads. Why? The seers, the rishis, were very wise. They realized that sometimes people in their ignorance might have issues with other people. People can be so quick to make a judgement; even if an incredibly beautiful thing has been written, that work might not be read because of some prejudice or other. Unfortunately, people will always have issues so better to leave this knowledge to be independent of any names. There has never been an individual who somebody hasn't had an issue with. They just don't exist. Sometimes the greater the individual, the more the people have issues with them. Better to leave them anonymous and then their range of influence can be greater. So even though the Upanishads are the crème de la crème of written wisdom, nobody takes ownership. That takes some level of genius. To create such a work, to express such marvelousness, and not take ownership of it? That in itself is a profound teaching. People of lower states of consciousness like to take ownership of everything.

So when you experience these Vedas, because they are shrutis what arises is poetry. It bubbles out as poetry and this poetry has a very profound impact because it has a frequency, a certain level of resonance. It is from where mantra yoga comes. By chanting that poetry, not just by intellectually decoding it, but by engaging in the practice of chanting it, one is using the mantra. The nature of reality is vibrational and when you are creating a certain vibrational environment within yourself, your physiology and the physiology of the nature around you responds in a certain way. This is verified by science now; the impact of sound, of music, on water, on trees, on children, on all of us, is profound.

The second part of the Vedas is the karma-mimansa, where very specific details on the technology to gain greater alignment with the fundamental laws of nature are given. The Vedic mantras have a rhythm to them because rhythms in nature that are repetitive create a greater resonance. It's a very specific, clear methodology; how to use certain sounds, certain movements, certain mudras, to gain unity with the laws of nature. They are not for glorification or the worship of nature. This is about tuning your consciousness so you can gain alignment with the laws of nature.

Toward the end of the Vedas is where the heart of the Yog-Vedantic tradition lies. This is where we find the Upanishads. The Vedas are subdivided into the Brahmanas, where the bija mantras start to arrive, and the Aryankas, where we find the Upanishads, the wisdom heart of the Vedas.

Vedanta has two meanings. The first being 'added at the end of the Vedas', very obvious as these are the works which are found at the end.

There were already suggestions of meditation present in the preceding Vedic teachings and this is the culmination of their realization, the synthesis of the whole knowledge, the supreme knowledge. Once you know this knowledge everything starts to be known. Once the knower starts to be aware of their own nature, then everything else starts to make sense. Everything. If the knower remains unknown, then all knowledge remains unhinged and ungrounded. For any knowledge to be relevant and fundamentally effective, it has to be grounded in a knower who is known. The Upanishads arose as the seers were practicing these Vedantic teachings. They were experiencing greater depths of their own being through utilizing this technology. Vedanta, the knowledge of Self.

Veda also means the field of knowledge which is not just within the books but beyond. The books are just an expression of that knowledge. It is important to realize that the yogic teachings are saying it is knowledge not just found in books. These are technologies, techniques, pointers for you to experience and gain access to the field of knowledge, the supreme knowledge which is dealing with the big questions, the fundamental questions of life. That is what the Upanishads are dealing with. Who am I? What is the nature of reality? The big questions in science are being answered here. The nature of fundamental particles, the nature of space, the nature of time, all answered here. The nature of consciousness, individuality, ego; all of this is being tackled in the Upanishads in an incredibly elegant and poetic manner.

So these teachings arise from a deep, inner realization for they are dealing with deep, complex questions. The characteristic of a genius is somebody who is able to express what appears to be incredibly complex in a seemingly effortless manner. Elegant simplicity, that's what you find in the Upanishads. They hold within them incredible levels of depth but they are expressed with incredibly poetic elegance; they just slip from your mouth:

> *Purnam adah, purnam idam,*
> *Purnat purnam udacyate*
> *Purnasya purnam adaya*
> *purnam evavashishyate*

You see how elegantly it just rolls off the tongue. In just these few lines they are talking about all the 'new' science, string theory, the Higgs field and the boson particle; talking about the unity of multiple dimensions of reality. What we are really discovering here in the Upanishads is that incredible genius starts to be experienced by beings who are practicing the yogic teachings.

The word upanishad has two meanings; first: *upa,* to come near, *nishad*, to destroy. It's like a declaration: come near me and I will destroy you. What it is really declaring is that if you come near to this knowledge, your ignorance starts to be destroyed. Nishad is destroying avidya. Upa, the proximity to this knowledge destroys all the incorrect knowledge. Any great knowledge ultimately has a destructive effect, destroying incorrect knowledge.

The second is: *upa* meaning Master, *nishad*, sitting near. Sitting near the feet of the Master. Again referring to the fact that these teachings were shared orally. For me that was one of the greatest ways I learned from my Master, if not the highest. Just sitting, being close to my Guru. There is a great value in that. Not thinking, not analyzing, not dramatizing, just being. Just being in close proximity to him.

So if we had to take a collective meaning of upanishad, it would be: knowledge which is transmitted through a live medium, through proximity, through reverberation, knowledge that has the potential of destroying the whole of ignorance within the individual's psyche. Knowledge by knowing which everything else starts to be known. Ultimately the whole yogic technology is about gaining greater and greater awareness of the Self. When the Self is aware and is intensely alive, then life becomes alive. For life can only be the way the experiencer is. Life is nothing but an experience the experiencer is having. There is no life outside the experiencer's field of consciousness. That's all life is. No one can experience anything outside their own field of consciousness. That's what experience fundamentally means, that which arises within the field of consciousness. Consciousness is what makes experience possible and through that consciousness the experience becomes known.

The Upanishads share the technology, the knowledge and the teachings which have the potential to clear ignorance out of our system. Within them there are many, many books but 108 is the agreed number. In actual fact there are a lot more. This is a body of profound knowledge, some are extremely technical and read more like science manuals than spiritual texts. From within these there are twelve principle Upanishads which form the central structure of the Vedantic knowledge and Isha Upanishad is one of the most beautiful. It is also the smallest and from where the mantra *Purnam adah...* comes. Many mantras used today came from these ancient texts. They do not talk about religions or belief systems The Upanishads are purely concerned with one thing: the nature of Self and the realization of it.

The knowledge found in the Upanishads is not just intellectual knowledge, it is also experiential practices. And the meaning of these mantras is never ever obvious. It is very important to realize that. When anybody reads the Upanishads, they are reading an interpretation and different interpretations of the Upanishads will have different meanings. These mantras are designed to be expounded upon, to be explored. They are not designed for you to devour and digest just like that. They are works of art which you have to dive into. Whatever level of knowingness you have awakened within yourself, that will be the depth of knowledge you discover. For this is not a static expression of knowledge. This is a dynamic awakening of knowingness.

There is a memory in the universe and your awareness expands and makes contact with that memory and draws knowledge from it. All knowledge which is evolutionary is ultimately derived from that field. Knowledge which is not evolutionary is just thought and that knowledge creates problems. It creates ideologies which are regressive and destructive in nature. But knowledge which comes from that inspired state has an evolutionary power embedded in it. When that knowledge is transmitted and shared and absorbed in the relative field of reality, it creates progression. Individuals who are engaging in that naturally find support from nature. You feel you are lucky, you feel supported. When you start accessing that field of knowledge, you will find the law of effortless ease starts to apply.

When we are exploring these scriptures, exploring the Upanishads, we are not just interested in the static value of that knowledge. We are interested in the dynamic deepening of knowingness. The wisdom is an algorithm which has the capacity to dismantle layers of avidya, ignorance, in you. You keep awakening to a deeper level of knowingness. The wiser the individual is, the humbler they will be because they realize that to be wise means to be dynamically knowing, not to be static in their knowing. When they meditate, something deeper is revealed and rises up from the great depth of their own silence; they realize then that they are always learning. And because they are always learning they remain forever relevant. Those who cease to learn become irrelevant and are pushed out by nature. For nature's command is to evolve and evolution requires deeper levels of knowing.

The Upanishads are meant to be explored, contemplated and meditated upon. We deepen our knowing as we revisit them again and again and again. We wake up every day with this great awareness in our heart, that we can discover something today which will totally transform our life and take it to the next level. The potential to transform our life, transform our consciousness and take it to the next level is always there. The Upanishads are deep fundamental truths, reverberating truths, arising from the great womb of silence with the power to transform our consciousness state. For the experiential value of the knowledge is always far greater than the intellectual understanding of the knowledge. The intellectual understanding is very relevant, very important, but the experience of the knowledge will always exceed the intellectual understanding. The intellectual understanding has to be there, but the experiential knowledge is where the dynamism arises. And that dynamism informs the intellect. It informs the intellect and corrects and expands its capacity. The intellect which encounters the knowledge in a static manner does not refine the experience of that knowledge; that intellect becomes stiff. That knowledge then becomes a burden.

The Upanishads invite us to explore the dynamism of that knowledge. We keep deepening, keep waking up to a deeper level of knowing, keep progressing, keep evolving. They have the potential to destroy the avidya, the grip of avidya, and that is why the wisdom of the Upanishads requires the technology of the yogic teachings. Without the technology, the knowledge becomes static. The evolution of the container is as important as the content; we must transform the container and keep giving it content. Keep the transformation flowing but also keep the information flowing. Shiva and Shakti, the yin to the yang and the yang to the yin.

Isha Upanishad

ॐ पूर्णमदः पूर्णमिदं पूर्णात् पूर्णमुदच्यते ।
पूर्णस्य पूर्णमादाय पूर्णमेवावशिष्यते ॥
ॐ शांतिः शांतिः शांतिः ॥

When we look at the whole expanse of the
Upanishads they are so amazing but
Ishavashaya is one of the ones that jumps out
because from here comes the great mantra:

> *Purnam adah, purnam idam,*
> *Purnat purnam udacyate*
> *Purnasya purnam adaya*
> *Purnam evavashishyate*

> *This is full and that is full, and*
> *this full has come out of that*
> *full. And even though this full*
> *has come out of that full, that*
> *full maintains its fullness.*

This is the invocation, a great declaration.
The whole Vedantic philosophy is right here.

The whole Vedantic worldview is contained right here within this mantra. The fullness of all dimensions of reality, whether manifest or unmanifest. *Purnam* meaning complete, whole. Another meaning for *Purnam* is shunya or the great void.

> *Purnam adah, purnam idam,*
> *Purnat purnam udacyate*
> *Purnasya purnam adaya*
> *Purnam evavashishyate*

Every Upanishad has a different invocation, a mantra, at the beginning. That mantra gives us a clue as to what that particular Upanishad is going to reveal to us, what it's going to share with us. You see, what we are exploring here is the fundamental nature of reality. The mantra itself is a declaration and will bring you to a deep level of equanimity which you need when entering any level of exploration. If you enter with any level of prejudice, any level of attachment to a certain position, any level of stress that "I must figure it out because if I don't figure it out then there is something wrong," then you are prone to come out having misunderstood it. That is why it starts with a declaration about the absolute perfection of all that there is, that there is nothing wrong. It is to create that deep equanimity. We are moving in the direction of knowledge and we are exploring this knowledge not because there is something wrong, that we need to get better, but because it is the fundamental purpose of existence. It is not based on any level of self-hatred. It is not based on any level of not being 'enough'. It is because the natural expression of being is to evolve.

A profound peace arises just in the chanting of that invocation. A certain experience of equanimity begins to arise in us. We find that the power of the mantra lies in how the sound is structured. It's quite amazing. The way the sound is composed, and the chanting of that sound, of that mantra, creates a certain response from the physiology.

Purnam adah, purnam idam,
Purnat purnam udacyate
Purnasya purnam adaya
Purnam evavashishyate

The moment this sound is invoked, irrespective of what is going on, there is a certain response which arises, and that response has a value of equanimity attached to it. The intention with this invocation is to really take the aspirant, the seeker, into that deeper state of equanimity. As I've said, if we approach knowledge with any level of pressure, we cannot access the true wisdom. What we access instead is information and information does not have the value of liberation. Information has a burdening value and that information breeds stress.

This invocation is one of the great Vedic mantras. It contains the whole philosophical understanding of the Vedas. The base understanding of it is that the creator is embedded in the creation. The Vedic view is that the clockmaker is in the clock. The clockmaker did not make the clock and then leave. The clockmaker is in the workings of the clock. *Purnam adah, purnam idam...* is really pointing directly at that. This is that and that is this, this is full and that is full and even though this full has come out of that full, that full is still full. That's why *purnam* is another name for zero. If you take zero out of zero, zero still remains.

In the relative field of reality, cause and effect have a very specific relationship. The cause undergoes a change, like when the matchstick is the cause of the fire. To create the flame, the matchstick goes through a change. So too, in the relative field of reality, the cause, as it produces an effect, will change. And that change, the force that creates that change, is then absorbed by the effect. The change itself is absorbed. The value of the change is directly proportional to the absorptive power of the effect. The effect absorbs the change and that is what then further propels the onward movement of the effect.

But here, when we are speaking of *Purnam adah, purnam idam*... the source does not change. It does not undergo any change. It maintains its changeless nature. What appears as the fullness remains whole; the cause does not undergo change. The cause remains changeless. It is very important for us to realize that that dimension of cosmic Being, that omniscient, omnipotent dimension is what? Changeless. That dimension of existence is subtler than space and time and it is not locatable in space and time. All space and time emerge from it; they are fully part of that emergence. The creator is in the creation.

So, even though this full is ever-changing, the relative field of reality is ever-changing, within that ever-changing reality the changeless is hiding. It's not somewhere else. It is just hiding at a subtler level of perception. That's what gives birth to what we call maya or illusion. Because the illusion which arises on the surface value looks dynamic, looks progressive, there is movement, yet it actually doesn't exist. The only thing that exists is the whole. *Purnam* exists. And that *purnam* shows up as *purnam adah* and as *purnam idam*. That and this are only two distinctions within the whole. It is just pointing it out. Who is pointing it out? The Self. The Self is pointing to two directions within its own nature. That is full and this is full.

When we say 'that', it means distance. When we say 'this', there is proximity. So this is whole and that is whole. And what is this? This is that. Because only that exists and only this exists. This and that are only two simple pronouns that we have used. But ultimately it is only the changeless that exists. All change is just rising up from the nervous system of the perceiver. As the perceiver refines, what they start to experience is the changeless.

Where there is birth and death and birth and death, that is change. Whether it is of the body or of the tree or of the mountain or of the butterfly, that birth and death is change. But from the Yogic perspective, it is illusion, *kala*. *Kala* is time, *kala* is illusion, *kala* is death. That it is an illusion does not mean that it doesn't exist; it exists. It is a whole existence but only on a certain level of perception. As long as the perception is limited to that degree, then it seems absolutely real. But, as the perception is refined, it loses its grip. And what is revealed is the whole. The wholeness reveals itself more and more and more. And the beauty of this wholeness is what? That it is infinite. It never ends. You don't ever say, "Oh, I get it all." You can't quantify it. You can't grasp the zero. You can grasp one or two. You can grasp the four fundamental forces of nature. But the zero you cannot quantify. You cannot hold it.

The fundamental nature of existence is not something that can be held or grasped. That's the challenge that the scientific community is now beginning to confront. How are the subatomic particles coming in and out of existence? From a great void, a dimension that cannot be measured. And what is that dimension? *Purnam adah*. It maintains its changeless nature and yet it shows up on the level of what we perceive as change. It is perceived as changing but it is actually changeless.

This is whole and that is whole. When one can really begin to realize that, then there is an incredible level of freedom which arises in the heart of the practitioner. When one can really grasp this understanding, one realizes there is just the whole that exists and what is arising is a play on the surface of it. Of course that play has to be respected. It has to be honored. It has to be treated as real. And that's what is explored in the rest of Isha Upanishad. We honor it, we are deeply grounded in the knowledge that this phenomenal reality, with its life and death and losses and challenges, is just on the level of our perception. It has to be treated with great respect, yes, but if the awareness only knows this to be the fundamental nature of reality, then it suffers incredible pain. That's what Buddha was talking about, *dukkha.*

This reality is impermanent. What is the relative field of reality? It is impermanent. And that which is impermanent does not exist. What does exist is that which is permanent. It is the whole that rises up and then falls back into the whole. Rises up and falls back. It is like the wave rising up and falling back into the sea.

The seer really wants us to understand this fundamental truth of life; if we can just know this then we are *Hari Om Tat Sat*. We are chill. We can encounter pain but within that pain we are all right. Because life is challenging no matter who we are. Behind all the malas and the temples, behind it all, there is always something to be learned, something to be understood, something to be faced. Yes? But once you realize the great play of it all, then you can enjoy the movie. Even the horror movie. Once you know it is just a movie, the horror movie can be fun. But for you to fully enjoy any movie, you first have to believe at that moment it is real. If you are sitting in a movie you have to suspend your disbelief, get invested in the characters and have a certain level of emotional involvement. There has to be juice. *Rasa*. The juice of life will not flow if you don't invest even in something as funny as Superman, the guy wearing his underwear over his slacks. You have to fully believe in him to enjoy the movie. To enjoy any movie, you have to fully commit to what's happening on the screen to get the best experience. This fine balance in you investing in the movie as being real while simultaneously knowing it's not is what gives it any value. And when the movie is over and you go out, it doesn't matter if it was tragic or disturbing or funny, it's like "Wow, that was brilliant."

This life that we are living right now is a work of art. And for you to really live it fully you have to believe it's real, just like the movie. If it does not feel real you will not really live it, you will not play the part, and then your life will end. Like when you come out of a movie and you want to have had a full experience, so it is in life. You want to have had all that you can experience, all that the Creative Intelligence has created, before it's over. The Creative Intelligence is the supreme director. It plays itself, it plays the part and then it is such a good director that it forgets that it's in its own movie. That's the beauty of it.

> *This is full and that is full, and this full has come out of that full. And even though this full has come out of that full, that full maintains its fullness.*

You can just meditate on that. It's so profound. When you meditate on this mantra a silence is reached. The thoughts are silenced. And what you are left with is the great experience of this play of life with all its varied emotions and challenges and laughter and tears. The yin to the yang and the yang to the yin.

So when we say that this is all an illusion, we are not saying that we should treat it as if it is nothing; that's a terrible mistake. Don't fall into that trap. It is important that you realize it's an illusion but then you act as if it is real. Because if you act as if it is not real, that's ignorance. The wise one knows it is not real, yet acts as if it is the only thing that exists. This is whole. This moment is whole. This person is whole. There is infinity hiding within every finite expression. For only the infinite exists. The finite has no existence; it is nothing but points within the infinite. What we call finite has no independent existence whatsoever. A wave in the ocean has no existence without the ocean. It is the ocean and it is the wave. It's a big mistake to think that the wave has an existence independent of the ocean. It has no existence whatsoever. Only the ocean exists. And that ocean rises up as the wave. That wave hides what? The ocean within itself. The infinity of the ocean. So from the infinite emerges a unified whole being, an individual walking, talking, having emotions, feelings, sensations. What exists is the whole. That is the only thing that exists. And the whole is playing within itself. *Purnam adah, purnam idam.*

Through our practice, we keep deepening that understanding, realizing that level of knowingness. I say realize because it is not something which you can completely grasp intellectually; the intellect is too limited to grasp the totality of this. But in your being, you can enliven this level of knowingness. It is knowing beyond the intellect. At the fundamental level of your being, when that knowing is enlivened, it is accompanied by a fearlessness. You can face the tragedy and the comedy. All the nine rasas, emotions, have to be experienced.

Once that deep knowing is there, then we can keep returning to it within our self. And what we find is a progressive realization of wholeness. That's evolution. What we call evolution is nothing but the progressive realization of the Is-ness, the progressive realization of our wholeness.

It's quite beautiful, isn't it? Quite phenomenal, such incredible genius. Just *purnam adah, purnam idam, purnat purnam udacyate*... and that's it. In the eighteen mantras that follow, the deepest philosophy of life is there. It is just beautiful, this Isha Upaniṣhad. Everything falls into place when you grasp this. When you really begin to grasp this on the level of knowingness, when your awareness is enlivened at that level where this knowledge becomes alive in you, then everything falls into place. That gives you the guts to truly live your life. It gives you the guts to watch the whole movie. It gives you the guts to experience the whole range of emotions, all the feelings, to be the hero and go on the journey. Without this knowledge you remain a tragic figure. When we get the courage to face life fully it will feel real, incredibly real.

It feels real and then where does it go? All these moments, where do they go? When you were five years old, where did that go? Where is that moment when you were a teenager with pimples? All those dilemmas which seemed so important, what to wear? What to do? Should I? Shouldn't I? Oh my god, all so real. Where should I go this Saturday? It all felt so real and where does it all go? Where do all the bodies that we see every day, where do they go? Where do the people we've known go? We've all experienced people we've loved or people we knew physically who are now not locatable in the body anymore. So where do they go? They go nowhere. They simply remain here. Because only here exists. Only the whole exists. And every expression is nothing but an expression of the whole. That is why everything is eternal. Every human being is eternal. Every soul is eternal. Because only the whole exists and if only the whole exists, then the whole cannot end. It has no end. It has no beginning. Look at the beauty in that.

You see, beginnings and endings are only within a certain level of perception; time is a level of perception. The Supreme Being, the whole, is subtler than time. It doesn't exist in time. It's not after time, it's before time. And it is not sitting somewhere else. It is just here because here is the only thing that exists. Nothing else exists, only pure consciousness. Everything else is movement within that, experiences within that. That is why this great Upanishad starts with this invocation and the following eighteen mantras just hammer it in.

The diamond is faceted from all aspects. It is explored fully. All doubts are removed. This profound truth really is so clearly expressed.

This is whole. And that is whole. Because there is only the whole. This and that are just two ways of us pointing to the whole. No isolated phenomenal reality has any existence. All isolated phenomenal reality is nothing but the whole expressing itself. What a great relief to realize that. We are so afraid of facing life, of the pain, of the emotion. Why? Because we forget the wholeness of it. We forget that this is all just a wave arising from the whole and soon this moment will disappear like all other moments. This movie will be over.

It is of great importance to realize that because it gives us incredible courage, we feel our most alive when we experience life in its intensity. When we shy away from it we feel half-dead, like a zombie. We long to experience life in its intensity but we are afraid of it. We want to love but we are afraid of that love, of losing that love, of getting hurt, of the pain. But when we know the great truth of *purnam adah, purnam idam, purnat purnam udacyate...* then our love becomes fearless. That's a great life, no? It's a life that the Vedic rishis, the seers, recommend. A life of fearless value.

So this Upanishad starts with this incredible mantra. Just be with it and it reveals itself. That's the beauty of these Vedic mantras, they reveal so much. Only eighteen mantras are here in this Upanishad but revealing such depth. If I am that, and that is the only thing that exists, then all that exists is me only. I am eternal, timeless. Yet I am the one who is born and I am the one who dies. I am the one who struggles and I am the one who cries. I am the eternally blissful, but I shed tears all the time. *Purnam adah, purnam idam.*

It's complete yet it rises up, the shakti rises up. There is dynamism in that. It's all just a play but it has to be treated as absolutely real. Every moment has to be approached as if it is the only moment that exists. And truth be told, it is the only moment that exists. Every individual should be approached as if they are the only one that exists. And the truth is, they are the only one that exists. Every flower should be approached as if it is the only flower that exists. And the truth is, it is the only thing that exists. When you embrace someone, embrace them as if it is the only moment that exists, and that body is the only body that exists, then that becomes a cosmic hug. Because the fact is, that is the only moment that exists. That body is the only body that exists. Only that exists in that moment. Everything is that. Every being is that. Every flower is that.

When we know that, we walk on this earth with eyes of supreme appreciation, with eyes of awe, eyes of gratefulness. And when we see the world with eyes of awe, wonder and gratefulness, the Mother reveals her charm to us, she reveals her great beauty. Otherwise she is shy. Our Mother is very shy. She hides. You have to look at her with a very specific attitude, only then she plays with you. And then she shows you her incredible beauty. But you have to adopt a certain attitude, otherwise you just wallow in the great wasteland created by the mind. It's a wasted life. No guts. A life of no guts we don't recommend. We must take on this attitude, look with appreciative eyes. Walk on this earth softly and gently and you will live much more deeply, much more intensely.

Whenever you find your mind getting worried about all the characters in your movie, all the roles you have to play, then you chant *purnam adah, purnam idam, purnat purnam udacyate…* and it deletes all thought. I guarantee it. You just chant it. Invoke that mantra. Move your awareness in the direction of the mantra and delete all thoughts. It fills you up with that deep knowledge of your own essential nature and of the nature of all else. For only the Self exists. That's what the great seers have declared and that's what we have verified from our own experience.

That's why the Vedic truths have stood the test of time. They are not belief systems. They don't need a propaganda machine to be shoved down people's throats. Whoever arrives at this teaching arrives of their own accord. They arrive on this path through their own longing, not by some manipulation, not through their parents pushing them. You arrive here because something in you awakens. It is the final frontier of a soul when it starts to encounter itself. Before that it is just wasting time.

This is full and that is full. That full has come out of this full. But even though that full has come out of this full, this full is still full. Cosmic consciousness. Cosmic stable consciousness is still full. What is cosmic consciousness? Unity. This is full. That is full too but it has drama. 'This' fullness has no drama. The drama always exists in 'that'; drama has a gap. When you are in bliss, you find there is no distance between you and it, you feel it so intimately. But when you are meditating, say in the morning, you find that thoughts are coming. We use the word 'coming', like they are coming from a distance, like a ghost swimming toward you. We find that when one really observes what we call toxicity, what we call drama, it is in 'that'. The drama only exists in 'that'. Cosmic consciousness is in 'this'. If you can establish 'this', then you are never reactive. For reaction can only exist when there is no 'this'. There is only 'that' dominating. The five-sensory observer reality is dominating, and 'this' is subservient; it is enslaved to the five-sensory nervous system. We must endeavour to reach the level where our experience truly is 'this', where 'this' is full.

ॐ ईशावास्यमिदँ सर्वं यत्किञ्च जगत्यां जगत् ।
तेन त्यक्तेन भुञ्जीथा मा गृधः कस्यस्विद्धनम्   ॥ १ ॥

1. *Ishavasyam idam sarvam yat kim ca jagatyam jagat tena tyaktena bhunjitha, ma grdhah kasyasvid dhanam.*

The Upanishads don't have titles. Their names come from the first word; the first word of the first mantra becomes the name of the Upanishad itself. So this is *Isha* Upanishad. Isn't that beautiful?

Isha, there is closeness to the sound of the word. When you say it, *Ishavasya*, do you not find the intimacy in that? *Isha*, so sweet, is it not? So close in its fullness. This is not an individual speaking. This is the cosmos but the cosmos can only speak through a channel of its own expression. The tree can only blossom through a flower which is an expression of its own self. If an individual perceives the flower existing independently of the tree, then they are extremely naïve. One can enjoy the flower, but if one starts to believe in the independent existence of the flower separate from the tree, then one does not enjoy the whole.

These really are such intoxicating mantras, *ishavasyam idam sarvam yat kim ca jagatyam jagat.* What it is saying is, all this, the Supreme Being, is embedded in this universe, in all that moves and even in all that doesn't move. Do you realize the brilliance of this? To know this without any hypothesis, without any 'maybe' or 'I think' or 'according to me' or 'as the Lord said', it's just sharing something without any ownership. There is no individual saying this because when an individual says it, there is an individuality embedded in it. Here there is no individual, there is just the Is-ness of the Cosmic Intelligence. It's simply saying whatever moves in this universe, and also that which doesn't move, is enveloped by the Supreme Intelligence. When you renounce this, when you don't have knowledge of this, then there is no wealth, *tena tyaktena bhunjitha ma grdhah kasyasvid dhanam.*

If you don't have the awareness of this, then where is the wealth? If you are always craving the other, then there is no wealth. It's like when we watch a movie and all the characters are up there on the screen. The screen is the movie, the characters on the screen are the movie, the light through which those particles are arriving and coming to life is the movie. The observer is that, the observed is that and the process of observing is that. If the observer does not have the knowledge of this Ishvara, then there is no wealth. Without this knowledge, this wealth, there is only the experience of poverty. Dhanam, wealth, *kasyasvid dhanam*.

If you are always craving the other, if everything you desire is other than you, then everything you actually are feels unsatisfactory. For craving is always directed away from oneself; one craves that which is outside of oneself. And in that craving is an inherent experience of unfulfillment. Whether it is sexual craving, food craving, fame craving, relationship craving, any kind of craving, one finds the experience of it is unfulfillment. One cannot crave without being unfulfilled. On occasion one might say as a figure of speech, just for fun, I am craving candy. But when one's actual experience is of real craving then one finds one is unfulfilled. All craving is backed by the feeling of unfulfillment. Hence, by that logic, the experience of fulfillment has to cancel out all craving. It's not the other way around. To be fulfilled is to cease craving.

There are some who propose that suppression of all cravings will result in fulfillment. No, it will only make the one who is craving more frustrated, more agitated, more aggressive. For you to start supposing that if you suppress your craving you will be fulfilled is you being an idiot. Unfortunately, if you are unfulfilled the only thing you know is craving. For what you are craving is to be fulfilled. That's what yoga is about: reaching fulfillment and not worrying about cravings. One who is fulfilled does not crave. Instead, one has a clarity to one's action, action relevant to one's evolution.

Another way of translating this mantra is that if one is not able to enjoy this natural truth, not able to understand that the Supreme Being is embedded in everything in this universe, then how can one enjoy any wealth? One will remain forever in distress. One doesn't have to believe in any of this, one can simply verify it with one's experience. One has to use one's rational mind. I always invite people to use their rational mind; contemplate deeply and reach your own verified conclusion which has been examined in the light of your awareness.

कुर्वन्नेवेह कर्माणि जिजीविषेच्छतँ समाः ।
एवं त्वयि नान्यथेतोऽस्ति न कर्म लिप्यते नरे ॥२॥

**2. *Kurvann eveha karmani jijiviset satam
samah evam tvayi nanyatheto sti na karma
lipyate nare.***

In the first mantra the seer spoke about the
fundamental nature of Self as being absolute
and the goal being the realization of that. Now
the seer says, a being who is backed by this
knowledge of indivisibility, who is experiencing
this unity, has to engage in this world fully for a
hundred years. Here the 'hundred years' is
really a metaphor for the full lifespan of an
individual human.

The seer explains that the only way to
realize the truth is by giving it your all here and
in the Now, throughout the full 'hundred years'
of your lifespan, the whole journey of your life,
irrespective of where you are in your biological
age. It is the only way to be, the only way for you
to experience freedom. Pour yourself totally
into this life, here and now, consistently for the
full 'hundred years' that you live here. For each
and every one of us will live for a 'hundred
years'. Our own 'hundred years'. Even from this

very moment, irrespective of what age we are, we will live a 'hundred years' more. A 'hundred' breaths more. You can call it a thousand years, you can call it five thousand years, you can call it one moment, you can call it five seconds. These are all just labels, that's all, a label, a tag. The seer is pointing out that irrespective of where you are, you have time. That's all you have. The only thing you have is time. That's why you are able to have this experience right now, because there is time.

But first one must realize this unity, this fulfilled state. Then one must live fully, doing one's work backed by this true knowledge. Here, the seer is making sure that the intellect is corrected and that there is no sense of escapism arising within the individual interacting with this knowledge. One must participate in life fully. Why? Because there is no other place to go. All the escapists who are trying to be in some other place, where they think life will be better, guess what? When they reach there, they will say the same thing. All these people who say they have issues with where they are, if you plant them in Hawaii after a while they will have issues in Hawaii. You plant them in a temple or at the beach, after a while they have issues there as well. The issues continue. The issues stay. One cannot run away.

This body, as it is appearing here in this very moment as the I, can only realize itself and gain liberation by engaging fully in the here and Now. Live totally and absolutely, while simultaneously being aware of the emptiness of all phenomenal reality. Within the full lifespan, the only way to experience nirvana is to engage in this life fully, here and Now, moment to moment. From the beginning of one's self-awareness to the moment one breathes one's last, there is no other path. There is only this path, the path of using this life in the fullest manner. There is nowhere else to go. Now just be with that for a moment.

To grasp the meaning that arises from this whole journey, one must first understand the absolute meaninglessness of it. For somebody who cannot cognize the emptiness of all phenomenal reality does not have the capacity to experience the meaning that exists beyond that of the five-sensory perception. This phenomenal reality, this interactive world, is simultaneously meaningful and meaningless. It is only when we interact with this relative field of reality fully, while maintaining an inner state of absolute detachment, that we can access supreme enlightenment both within and without. You interact, you serve, you love, you play fully, only then you are complete. The Yog-Vedantic teachings are not about escaping or denial of the relative field of reality but rather a full jump into the possibilities of what it means to be. For someone who is truly established in this awareness, in the profound emptiness of all reality, yet engages in it as if it is supremely full, no karma attaches to them.

Within that living of a full life, the question arises: what does it mean to live? We seem to be one of the only species on this planet that asks it, and I stress the word seem. It only seems so, it might not be so, it might not be the absolute truth. Maybe the whales are asking the same question, the dolphins and the monkeys too, who knows? But from our perspective we seem to be the only species which can ask this question and try to answer it. What does it mean to live? What does it mean to be? It's a very important question, what does it mean to be?

You are born and you die and in between is what we call life. Within that is the seeking of a certain level of fulfillment, for fulfillment has such an impact on the human mind. The human mind seems to be designed to seek fulfillment. Yet we find the state of fulfillment to be very rare. Unfortunately, only a few individuals are radiating the state of fulfillment, irrespective of their state of accumulation, irrespective of their labels, irrespective of what they do or don't do. So one of the common themes of life is seeking fulfillment. If we really observe, we find life is just happening and most people are in denial that they have no control over this flow of life, progressing at lightning speed toward their eventual annihilation. They are in denial of that. They keep themselves busy, distracted. Does a busy life mean a life lived fully? No. The only way to experience a full life is through engaging with the manifest dimension of reality. For there is no other world to go to. This is a very profound declaration right at the beginning of this Upanishad: I am, that I know. Before any labels are attached to the I am-ness, there is just the I am-ness. And this I am-ness is found in this life, for that is where we are, in this life as these bodies.

If you buy into some religious ideologies based on a misinterpretation, what they are selling is a seat in a transcendental future; they teach that heaven is somewhere else, in some other realm. This is just a decoy for the ego to postpone liberation. The mind identified with the ego is constantly in a chronic state of postponement: postponing cognition, postponing truth, postponing freedom. Something else is always more important right now. It's fascinating, even though the only thing that the being seeks is liberation, there is always something more important in the moment than that freedom. Here, the seer warns us that there is no other way. There is no other world. Let go of that fantasy. Let go of this idea that you are just doing time here and there will come a moment when this time ends and you will find yourself in some sort of blissful golden garden. If you cannot locate the blissful golden garden here, forget about it; it doesn't exist for you. You are incapable of discovering the capacity within yourself to cognize the freedom that is within this life. For all meaning is self-manifested. All vision is self-created. The freedom within this life is when you interact with it, when you engage with it fully.

Backed by the correct knowledge, one must live fully because there is no other place to go. One cannot go anywhere else if one does not fulfill one's role here. There is only here. You must look at this, this very moment. Not somewhere else but right here and right now. Ask: am I interested in emancipation? Am I interested in liberation? Am I interested in freedom? For if I am interested in liberation, it can only have any relevance if it is within the context of this life. If I have to wait for freedom when I am no longer in this life, then that freedom is useless. Freedom is only relevant within the domain of I am. And when I am freedom, there is brilliance.

We all know this from our own experience. You know that there comes a time when you reach a destination, physically and inwardly, it becomes clear to you, there is no other place to run to. Every soul has to reach that position in its life where they realize there is no other place to go. Everything must be faced here. The only way you can be free is when you can bring this freedom into the interactive reality and you can spend your whole life, from now till your last breath, engaging fully from that place of absoluteness. There is no heaven elsewhere. Get cozy with that fact.

There is this idea, this delusional idea, that there is death and there is some extraordinary life after death. No. There is only life. There is no death. When there is no death there is no life after death. There is just life. And how is that life? It is just the way you are here. It's a fact, you are not going anywhere. Get used to it. It's a liberating realization. You are not going anywhere at all. This is a very deep realization. As you realize that, that is the beginning of freedom, that there is no other place than here. The other place is an illusion. For it's all happening within the field of consciousness. So, the only way to be liberated is if you are liberated where? Right here.

Backed by this knowledge, we must act fully, play our roles to our fullest capacity, to the best of our abilities, without getting attached to any expectation, to any result. We simply do our best. This is a very powerful mantra. It explains the only way for us to experience the Divine is here. Not after we die. We must meet the Divine here. There is no life after death. There is just life and that life can only be the way you are, here and Now. That is what the seer is saying. The only way you can taste liberation is by living your whole life fully, engaging fully, here and Now. While at the same time, being established at the level where there is just silence and the Absolute, no shape and no form.

असुर्या नाम ते लोका अन्धेन तमसाऽवृताः ।
ताँस्ते प्रेत्याभिगच्छन्ति ये के चात्महनो जनाः   ॥३॥

3. *Asurya nama te loka andhena tamasa vrtah tams te pretyabhigacchanti ye ke catmahano janah.*

The universe really got passionate in this mantra: sunless are those worlds without light, enveloped in an eternal gloom. Sunless, enveloped in an eternal gloom. Worlds manifested and entered by the souls that deny the truth of their own nature. They are the ones that go there. It's really dramatic stuff. Powerful. Asurya, meaning demonic state of consciousness, asurya state. Sunless, absence of illumination, full of gloom. Gloom is in full supply. There are people like that, people who have an endless supply of gloom. They are the ice cream vendors, the kabuliwalas, of gloom. They show up and instead of dispensing treats, they throw gloom around. They rejoice in spreading gloom. We are not interested in that. We are not interested in making people suffer. Who is interested in that? Those souls that deny the truth of their own nature, who are in passionate denial, they create the worlds without sun, the worlds of eternal gloom. And then they enter them.

The universe is quite brilliant here. Remember, this is not a person saying this, this is the universe saying it to itself. The souls which are in denial, in passionate denial about the truth of unity, the inherent nature of love, not somebody who doesn't know this but is in denial of it, they create worlds where there is no sun. Sunless worlds filled with gloom. They create them for themselves and their fellow beings and then they enter them.

You see, the mind creates the dream and then instead of watching the dream from the outside knowing that this is something it is creating, it enters the dream and then witnesses the dream from the inside out. The dream, the dreamer and the characters within the dream are all expressions of the conscious state of the individual dreaming. Say you dream of Rishikesh, you find yourself walking in the streets of Rishikesh, or maybe you have a dream about running through the forest. Your mind has manifested this forest and planted your individuality inside this forest, then you start to run in this forest, running away from a demon your mind has also manifested in this forest.

You don't know in the dream that you are dreaming, you only realize that when you wake up. That's why people don't like to have bad dreams. For the duration of the dream it feels like their neurological and physiological reality. It feels real. If you measured the brain synapses in that individual at that time, they would be firing stress. They would have high levels of cortisol.

So these souls manifest gloomy worlds for themselves and their fellow beings and then they enter these worlds together. Sunless, meaning no illumination, sunless worlds. Denying awareness. It just takes one person to make a gloom palace and go inside and then other people join them there. Now these people inside the gloom palace all start talking about how gloomy their lives are.

For the gloom merchants, tamas dominates their thinking and their intellect and their logic. From this tamasic state, they roam around in this world, even after they die. That's where we get the idea of hell. For when does one go to hell? After one dies. But this hell only exists in the field of one's consciousness. I see people who have done this, cultivated this habit of gloom for themselves for years and years and years. Just a little pinch, a little nudge, is all it takes to create a gloomy world in which to build a gloom palace where they can live. As soon as they feel they have a little problem, it affects their energy. They go right back into the gloom palace. Why? Because it's familiar. It's so familiar to their mind, their way of being, it feels safe, like it's their resting place. They hate it but they know it. Plato talked about it in his allegory of the cave, the shadows on the wall of the cave being the manufactured reality. So the human condition is forever bound to the impressions that are received through the senses. "Even though I hate it, at least I know it."

One has to be ever vigilant; one must use the key, unlock the door, and step out of the gloom palace. Use the key of your sadhana, your practice, apply it diligently, open the door and step out. Stay out in the sunlit world, the world of illumination. One must not build a gloom palace. But if one does and finds oneself in it, then one must know one can step out anytime one wants. One always has the key. One cannot lose the key to this gloom palace. The doors are never locked from the outside; the doors are always locked from the inside. There is no lock on the outside and because it locks from the inside, it can only be opened from the inside. If you want to stay in the gloom palace you can, no problem, because only you can get yourself out of the gloom palace. No one else can take you out of the sunless world of eternal doom and gloom.

However, after consistent practice amrita develops, soma. An inner illuminated state starts to be experienced and then you can open the gloom door and come out. One must not ever say that somebody else put them in the gloom room. For no other person is capable of creating a gloom palace inside your head. Only you can do that. Whatever is happening in your life you can choose how you deal with it. You create your heaven and you create your hell. The universe is saying it right here, that those souls, those expressions of me which are in denial of me, create for themselves worlds without sun, fill them up with gloom, enter and roam around in them when they are in the body and even after the death of that body. They roam in the gloom alone and then they invite other people in too. It's a statement of fact and quite brilliant.

अनेजदेकं मनसो जवीयो नैनद्देवा आप्नुवन्पुर्वमर्षत् ।
तद्धावतोऽन्यानत्येति तिष्ठत् तस्मिन्नपो मातरिश्वा दधाति ॥४॥

4. *Anejad ckam manaso javiyo nainad deva apnuvan purvamarsat tad dhavato' nyan-atyeti tisthat tasminn apo matarisva dadhati.*

This is fascinating, one of the names for the manifest world in Sanskrit is *jagat*, meaning that which moves. And here, brilliantly, the cosmos has used the word *anejad*, that which doesn't move. So the Self is motionless. The Supreme Being is motionless. All motion arises within it but the Supreme Being is motionless. Yet it is swifter than the mind. Before the mind can arrive at any location, the Supreme Being is already there, faster than the fastest. Those who run after it cannot find it. The faster you run, the faster it moves.

This mantra is explaining that the Supreme Being is motionless. Not meaning impotency or the absence of passion and creativity but motionless meaning that dimension of being that is subtler than space and time. For motion means what? Change. The body moves, yes? Motion means change of location; that is motion. If the Supreme Being is not locatable at a single point, but is located in all points, then how can it move? This is incredible knowledge. The Supreme Being is swifter than the mind. For the fastest thing that we have access to is our mind. It's faster than light. It is faster than all things that can be perceived. The fastest traveling thing is the mind. Right now your mind can be anywhere you want. Right now you can think about being in America or France, or on Saturn or Jupiter. And the Supreme Being is faster than the mind. All that one perceives is the Self, motionless, changeless. All change is within the Self. The Supreme Being in its essential nature is changeless, yet it favors change and is faster than the mind, faster than the senses.

Even the devas cannot overtake the Self. Deva has two meanings: the celestial being, coming from light, that which illuminates, and it's also the name for the senses. The Supreme Being is faster than the senses, faster than the celestial beings. One experiences one's individualized incarnation of the Divine, of Ishta, but the Supreme Being is even faster. For the Ishta is also an expression within the Supreme Being. For there to be a celestial expression, there has to be a background in which the celestial expression plays itself. What we call the astral realm has to have a background, a background on which all perception, all that is perceived on any level, the grosser level of existence or the astral level of existence, can be experienced. But even when we are experiencing the astral realm, the Supreme Being is subtler than that. For the astral realm is an expression within that infinite field of being. Since the Supreme Being is motionless, it is locatable at any point and because it is motionless, all motion is within it.

As the individual jiva, the soul, has access to greater and greater levels of the Supreme Being, you will find that it starts to become motionless. When we say motionless, it does not mean that the being is not creative. No, they become more creative, more loving, more kind, more alive. Yet there is a changeless quality that starts to arise in the individual, a timeless quality. That individual naturally starts to take on a greater and greater ageless quality. They can no longer be broken by a little change in their circumstances. They become less fragile and more stable.

This whole idea that when one gets more and more spiritual, goes deeper and deeper, one becomes more and more fragile is totally crazy. As you move within, and become more and more your true Self, you become less fragile. Sensitive yes, but sensitivity is not fragility. Sensitivity which is fragile is not being sensitive. It is narcissistic. It means you are fundamentally concerned about me, myself and I. It's all I'm feeling this or I'm feeling that. Who is feeling what? Me. I am. This is just a greater degree of narcissism; this we are not interested in. We must not support this kind of fragile sensitivity.

The Supreme Being is subtler than the devas. So when you go to your subtler consciousness it is not a fragile experience. Any spiritual experience which is 'fragile' is irrelevant. This is not a spiritual sign. One can confuse sensitivity with fragility but they are not the same thing. Because of their wrong knowledge, that to be sensitive means to be fragile, people have confused the two. "I'm very sensitive," they say. They are not. It is the pseudo-culture which has made sensitivity a sign of weakness; we have numbed down our sensitivity because to be sensitive means to be dramatic, to be bothered by life. We have to realize that sensitivity, true sensitivity, is a sign of great strength. It is nothing to do with being bothered about anything. We are interested in that sensitivity which is grounded. When the sensitive individual has access to their true sensitivity they will not be fragile. They will become stronger, more and more indestructible. Sensitivity, in its most refined value, is compassion. A compassionate person can face the pain and bring their love into it. Compassion is not being bothered by life. It is you transcending that location where you are bothered by life.

As you go deeper within yourself, as the jiva has access to the Supreme Being, what has to happen? Motionlessness. Motionlessness is what? Maintaining the ever-changing dimension yet being changeless. That you can be trusted fully, absolutely, totally by the universe. There is something so marvelous about an individual who is changing, yet you find they are also changeless. That is love. That is the only love. Otherwise there is no love. For love to be there, there has to be the changing and the changeless together. The changeless anchors love and the changing gives one permission to be free. The changeless kills insecurity. Kills it. Shoots it right in the head. Boom. True love kills insecurity. Kills it dead. In the presence of true love there cannot be insecurity. But true love does not make the insecure secure. If there is insecurity there is not love, there is only thinking. For one to experience true love, one has to experience within oneself the changeless amidst the ever-changing.

The essential nature of the Supreme Being is motionlessness and the greater your access to that, to the changeless, the greater stability you will have. What we call insecurity is a phenomenon which is experienced by an individual trapped in the ever-changing dimension of reality. That is insecurity. You look for security, for something that does not change, yet you find that everything you see is ever-changing. So what happens? You feel greater and greater insecurity. Then when one is around the quality of changelessness one feels all right, one feels safe, secure. But the moment you start feeling that you are safe and secure, you can also feel the possibility that you are unsafe. Why? Because it is only an idea, 'I am safe'. For once that idea is there, there can also be the opposite idea, 'I am not safe'. Then you feel insecure.

Only when you are stable can you start to have a great life. You are no longer craving,

craving, craving, looking for the next fix. Spiritual window shopping. People who only have access to the ever-changing phenomena are just shopping around for that experience or this experience. Life is not just a shopping center but those who don't have access to the Supreme Being, to that motionlessness, are only interested in the shopping center. They don't know what they are looking for but they are shopping nevertheless. When one can start to access within oneself the changeless, motionless Being, then one can start having access to it in the external dimension of one's life. When I say changeless, I mean timeless. You can start to locate those people with that quality. You can trust that person fully, totally, absolutely. It's not you who is trusting; it's the universe that can trust that person because that person has a greater quality of the universe within them. The changeless is supporting the ever-changing phenomena. Otherwise one remains unstable.

What we call the universe is an ever-moving phenomenon, ever-changing. If there was no change, there would be no time. For there to be time, there has to be a timeless presence which supports the experience of time. If you draw a line from A to B that is time; time is equal to distance over speed. You divide the distance by the speed and you get the time, the measurement of change. That is what we call time. All time is nothing but a measurement of change.

No change. No time. You can verify this. If someone gets locked up in solitary confinement, they start to lose all concept of time. Why? Because inside the space they are confined nothing is changing. That's why the yogis used to go into the cave. After a while you lose the concept of time. Friday, Saturday, Sunday, it's all the same. Then you realize how 'made up' it all is. People get excited because it's the weekend. Their whole life revolves around the weekend; waiting for the weekend. But it's just a 'made up' thing.

So what we call time is a measurement of change. No change, no time. Because the Supreme Being is subtler than space and time, there is no change. Changeless is timeless. Timeless is changeless. And because the Supreme Being is timeless it can be accessed at any moment. The more one has access to that dimension within oneself, the more timeless one gets. Timeless in the sense that one's knowledge is not limited by time, not limited by one's physiological age, anymore. Timeless in the sense that one is no longer insecure, no longer looking for the changeless in the ever-changing phenomena. If any individual is insecure, then it is a clear sign that they don't have access to the dimension of truth within themselves.

If your practice has any validity, then you have to become less and less insecure. Any insecurity that is arising in your consciousness is just a bluff of the lower mind. If you engage with it, then you will feel insecure. You have to recognize that that is just the lower mind and not engage with the melodrama. You have to access the non-changing Self, which can be accessed at any time for it is beyond time. Something which does not live in the dimension of time cannot be accessed in time, meaning what? It cannot be accessed in the future. It can only be accessed Now.

As you gain more and more access to the Supreme Being within yourself, it does not mean you will not move. You will move. You will have more ecstasy. The Kundalini will move in you. You may experience your body jerking, you may dance in ecstasy. All this is an expression of the motionless within. We are not speaking of motionless as in stagnant. Motionless here means non-changing. As one achieves this, one becomes more and more secure within oneself. One is less dramatic. One is not afraid. For all fear is fear of the unknown. Fear of losing the known. For if one is absolutely certain that there is no death, why would one be afraid of death? For one to be afraid of death, one is afraid of what? Losing the known.

First is the fear of losing the known and then comes the fear of the unknown. But as we gain access to our own Supreme Being then naturally we gain greater and greater stability within ourselves. One's internal experience becomes more and more stable. The changeless maintains. One raises one's deserving power. True deserving power cannot be raised by a person who does not have access to the changelessness within themselves. An ever-changing person has no deserving power.

So, the meaning of this mantra is that the Self is motionless, the Supreme Being is motionless and subtler than space and time. All life is maintained through it. All life. The last part here is *matarisva dadhati*. There are two meanings to *matarisva*. Mata is the individual soul, atman. Mata is also mother. So the meaning is also, the Cosmic Mother births everyone through the Supreme Being. Look at the beauty in that. Mata, the Divine Mother, supported by the Supreme Being, rises up and through her womb, births everything into creation and then sustains it through her breath. Shiva and Shakti. Shiva, the Supreme Being, the eternal field of silence; Shakti, the great Mother arising from this and birthing all into existence. Birthing it and sustaining it. The mother principal arises from this changeless being. The divine feminine principal arises from her; from her womb she manifests and she sustains the ever-changing phenomena. This is so profound.

तदेजति तन्नैजति तद्दूरे तद्वन्तिके ।
तदन्तरस्य सर्वस्य तदु सर्वस्यास्य बाह्यतः   ॥५॥

5. *Tad ejati tan naijati tad dure tad vad antike tad antarasya sarvasya tad u sarvasyasya bahyatah.*

This is so wonderful. The Supreme Being moves. *Tad ejati tan naijati...* and it moves not. *Tad dure tad vad antike...* it is so far and so near. This is incredible, this mantra, so deep there is no bottom to it. It moves and it moves not. It is so far and it is so near. *Tad antarasya sarvasya tad u sarvasyasya bahyatah...* it is within all this and also outside all this.

True silence within cannot be broken. There is no actual difference between inside or outside but for one to really know this, one must first go within. One cannot know this without going within. For one to have access to not being within, one must first go within truly, fully, absolutely.

When we say 'within' what do we mean? Where does one go? Where do you go? To the heart? To the mind? If you cut the body open, do you find anything 'within'? No. Right now, where are you? Are you within or without?

What this mantra is saying is that the Supreme Being is both within and without. So when you go within you find all that is outside is there, within and without. So close and so far. It moves and it moves not. It is all this and all that. It doesn't move and yet it moves. Like when we observe nature, we find that she is always still yet always moving. We find the changeless and the ever-changing coexisting in perfect equilibrium, perfect harmony.

It moves yet it moves not. It is so far yet it is so near. It is all this and it is all that. There is a great ecstasy in longing but we must cultivate this longing. There is a secret I will tell you, the Supreme Being, God, Goddess, Absolute, the Divine, whatever you want to call it, is very near to you. But you must cultivate the longing, as if it is so far away. When we are in a devotional state, we are in a deep state of longing and we find that it feels so far away. But when that longing starts to reach a certain stage, then it brings it near. Yogis call it mumukshutva. Mumukshutva is a unique kind of desire which we must cultivate. It is the desire for the Sacred. Desire for Divine Mother. Desire for the Supreme Being. Desire for self-realization. One must cultivate this strong desire for liberation.

The cultivation of this liberation brings it closer. It moves and yet it doesn't move. We can verify it in our own experience. When we go into our deeper, subtler states we find these two phenomena merge and they are indistinguishable. When you go into subtler states of consciousness within yourself, you will experience it as a profound stillness and, at the same time, as profound movement. A movement unparalleled. You will feel things are moving inside of you like you have never experienced before.

When we go into our own subtler dimension, in our meditation or in our kriya, we find that we get into this profound stillness at the center. But we also find that when we get into that center something starts to move and this movement is unparalleled. It is unlike any other movement we have ever experienced. Because all the movement that we have experienced before is a movement between two points. This is the first time we start to experience a movement of consciousness within itself. When our perception refines at that level, we find that all that we perceive is the consciousness moving within itself. For consciousness cannot move anywhere else; it can only move within itself. From the perspective of the Cosmic Mother, all this movement is within herself. When you get into that state it can surprise you, "What's this going on here? What am I seeing?" You are experiencing that level where there is no difference between movement and no movement. They are not opposite to each other. It's like deep sea diving. When you go down deep, you find there is movement; it's not just at the surface. This movement has the quality of the ocean. The ocean is moving within itself.

So near and yet it is so far. That is the experience of the devotee. A true disciple, a true devotee, has this dual experience of the Divine. This incredible intimacy, this proximity, and simultaneously a great distance. The Sacred, the Divine Mother, is so close and yet so far. So, the devotee maintains a humble nature, always being in service and receptive; never taking the proximity for granted. For the proximity and distance coexist. You can verify it from your own experience. With my Guru I felt like this, so close, yet so far, simultaneously. The intergalactic universe, so close yet so far. So far, yet so near. There's a great ecstasy in that. Distance and proximity coexisting in the

Supreme Being, the Divine Mother. There is no greater love than this love. This is the only true love. It is within and it is without.

So, the Yog-Vedantic teachings are not saying that this world is meaningless. They are saying that this world of shape and form is also an expression of that Supreme Being within. They are saying this world must be experienced in its fullness. It must be celebrated in its fullness. It must be realized in its fullness both within and without.

यस्तु सर्वाणि भूतान्यात्मन्येवानुपश्यति ।
सर्वं भूतेषु चात्मानं ततो न विजुगुप्सते ॥ ६ ॥

6. *Yas tu sarvani bhutani atmany evanupasyati sarvabhutesu catmanant tato na vijugupsate.*

He who begins to see himself starts to see himself everywhere.

When one sees oneself everywhere, one cannot hate. All hatred starts to dissolve. As I have said often, all love is directed toward oneself, and all hatred that one feels is directed toward oneself too. When one hates somebody else, that hatred is a direct reflection of one's hatred for oneself, of the struggle within oneself. For it is not possible to be at peace and to hate somebody, the one who hates cannot be at peace. It is not possible for you to have issues with somebody and to be at peace. To have issues with somebody else is a reflection of you having issues within yourself. When one truly sees oneself then one cannot harbor hatred. When one constantly sees all existence in the Self, and the Self in all existence, one cannot hold on to hatred. For one to harbor that feeling, one is in conflict within oneself. That is not a state of clarity. That is a state of neurosis.

It feels so good to not hate anybody. It's much more fun to have nobody in the world you have issues with. It's amazing. You get up and wow, you don't have any issues with anybody. Wonderful. If you have issues with people, then it's not possible to be enlightened. Not possible. As one starts to see oneself fully, the hatred gives way to love. One does not hate one's life. And as hatred drops, love happens.

Vijugupsate. It's a really wonderful word, a beautiful word. It is referring to the experience of shrinking, contraction. So, building on that truth in the 5th mantra, that the fundamental nature of Self is all-pervading, non-local, expressing itself within the context of experience and the experience as a localized value of self, it says here that when one sees one's Self in all existence and sees all existence within one's Self, then how can one ever contract? There cannot be *vijugupsate*, contraction; one does not go in the direction of shrinkage. As I've said, evolution naturally means diversification, the individuality expanding, diversifying. Within the context of the experience of love and the context of the experience of life, diversification is the law of evolution. When we say diversification what we are really saying is expansion, meaning: not the ever-repeating known. Diversification is the entry to the unknown within the realm of one's own experience. This entry to the seemingly unknown, within the realm of one's own experience, is the movement of the seemingly individual consciousness in the direction of its own greater Self.

As this diversification of consciousness, this expansion, is taking place, the seemingly other is coming within the realm of one's own Self. When it does so, fear is not possible because fear is always of the unknown, the other. People are so afraid of being alone but in their aloneness the only thing they are afraid of is somebody else. In that aloneness, that apparent silence, it's as if there is somebody else there, somebody unknown.

From a very young age, alone in a dark room or in the forest, the fear is always that there is somebody else there. If you really examine the fear, the fear is always of something else, that there is something out there. Have you ever gone in the water and something touches your foot? People freak out when that happens if they can't see what it is, "Ah! Something touched me." But when the seer starts to see all existence within the Self, and the Self within all existence, then how can there be any fear? How can there be any shrinkage? How can one become isolated? Become secretive? Alone? Alone in the context of moving in the direction of contraction. *Vijugupsate*, such a beautiful use of the word.

Any experience of karma, any experience of being bound by avidya, bound by ignorance, is accompanied by the sensation of shrinkage, of being small, of being pathetic. Any thought which has the value of ignorance attached to it, thought which might be arising from a sense of competition, a sense of lack, of insecurity, of whatever your 'issue' may be, will have this sensation of being small, of being weak. Then, no matter how much you do, how into the flow you are, doing your very best, once this mind value bound by ignorance rises, you will start to think that you're not doing enough and the feeling of smallness, of shrinkage, will be there.

Similarly, where you start to feel bigger, better than everybody else, the value of shrinkage will accompany that too. If you really check in with yourself, you will feel the stress in there. For this feeling of stress, of fear, of comparing oneself, to arise, there has to be 'other'. For there to be conflict there has to be 'other'. For you to be conflicted within yourself there has to be 'other'. You have to be split within yourself. This is how most people live, always concerned with the 'other'. And the deeper you look, the more you realize you have no clue what is going on.

Most people are just keeping themselves busy. They have no clue what is going on in life. We have got to stop and really question this. Why are you doing whatever it is you are doing? Because that is what you must do? Why? Because that is how you pay the bills? But why must you pay the bills? Why have we created a society based on that? Based on a life that revolves around paying the bills? Why do we think that we can find the truth in our work? People have become obsessed about it. But deep down inside, they know that it is all meaningless. Once the meaninglessness of it all is understood, then the true meaning can be cognized. All we have here is a crisis of meaning, a projection, an obsession, a perversion of value. For we are giving something a meaning that it doesn't really have and so we are bound to be in a state of conflict, a state of stress. We are bound to be in a state of pompous, inflated ego, giving ourselves supreme self-importance.

People are stressed every day. When little things happen they freak out and they are not even aware they are being dramatic. They think there is something really big going on, something really important, and they really believe in it. For you to be in any state of stress, any state of manipulative thinking, then clearly you are stuck in a very perverse sense of isolated identity. When these thoughts come, thoughts about how to manipulate your life, how to figure out what others want from you, how to figure out if they like you or not, if they love you or not, so much busyness, it's just a way for the ego to not face the truth. It is a coping mechanism of the existential crisis that really is at the base of an individual's experience, a crisis over what this really means. Because somewhere deep inside, there is this realization, this voice, that all of this means nothing at all.

People die every day and life keeps on going. Nobody bats an eyelid. And you know it. Your body ends but Starbucks will still be open. People will still be standing in line complaining. Our experience of death is of death of the other.

Not of our own death but death of the other. We ourselves have no clue of what it means to die and therefore we are afraid of death; we only understand life in the context of the 'other'. But life goes on. People forget.

Somewhere, lurking, there is always the question, what does this all mean? The human ego is so terrified of this that it projects false meanings, false ideologies, and keeps itself occupied. Always busy and always reactionary. There is no response, just reaction to external stimuli. One's whole life becomes reactionary. And whenever this reaction occurs, there you find a shrinkage, a moving away from evolution, from expansion, from that state of unity.

So this crisis, this pressure that one feels, is to try to find some meaning in the circus that is life. Then this idea is created that there is somebody else, something else. But only when you can realize the fundamental emptiness of all phenomena can you experience any level of meaning in this life. As long as you do not realize the fundamental absolute nothingness of all phenomena, you are caught in the delusion. All of this, all that we surround ourselves with, ultimately means nothing. Your body means nothing. How you look means nothing. What you have means nothing. What you know means nothing. What you don't know means nothing. It means nothing at all. Try that on for a while.

Even your thoughts mean nothing. Any thought you have, just realize it means nothing. Just take away the meaning from that thought. You can practice it right now. Any thought you have, give it no meaning whatsoever. We are so busy creating all kinds of fantasies. But what if you take away the meaning from all thought? Only then can you learn to use the mind. Everything that floats around in your mind, you give a meaning to it, "Oh, I was thinking..." Who cares what you were thinking? Why not take a break from trying to locate the meaning of life within the limited capacity of your mind? Just take a break right now.

Only when you can take a break from that obsessive thinking, that obsessive need to attach value to every little thing that arises in the field of your awareness, can you begin to discover the power of the mind. Only then you can begin to discover the true meaning. No meaning can be experienced without experiencing the meaninglessness of it all. For ultimately, all phenomena are empty. All phenomena. All shape and form. This is what science is now proving, that all shape and form are nothing but the dance of emptiness. So, if all shape and all form, all phenomena in your phenomenal experience within this realm of shape and form, are predominantly a dance of emptiness then all shape and all form, all phenomena in your phenomenal experience within this realm of shape and form, are empty. That includes the experience of your body and the experience of this world; all are fundamentally empty. Now you be with that.

If you cannot find the meaninglessness of it all then you cannot find meaning. Understand the polarities coexist. Without Shakti there is no Shiva. Without Shiva there is no Shakti. Without yin there is no yang. Without the night there is no day. Without timelessness there is no time. Without death there is no life. Without falling there is no getting up. If you want to get up, you must learn how to fall. If you can face the absolute meaninglessness of the phenomenal world, face it. I am not talking about a state of apathy, which is nothing but the ego stuck in a state of crisis. I am talking about a courageous declaration, this cognition, this understanding, of the meaninglessness of the phenomenal world. Only then can there be meaning to all aspects of life. Without that there is no meaning.

This is something you can apply right now. Catch yourself in that movement of isolation. If you don't, you can never set yourself free. Without catching yourself, you cannot achieve freedom. The moment you catch yourself, in that very moment, the possibility of you setting yourself free opens up. If you do not catch yourself, you are enslaved by 'other'. Your idea of 'other'. If you can be with this for just 20 to 30 minutes every day, that there is no 'other', there is only yourself, that this whole phenomenal world is absolutely meaningless, I guarantee you this: you will change. You cannot remain the same once you know this. I guarantee it. Once you understand the meaninglessness of it all, you are no longer attached to any isolated value. The being who is experiencing the Self in all directions, one's Self in all existence and all existence in one's Self, is in a state of non-attachment. This is self-referral consciousness, meaning consciousness that knows itself. Then when you can let go, you can have it all. Understand that.

So, when the seer sees itself in all existence, and all existence in itself, in that moment all judgment drops. Those thoughts that show up when you are alone, be aware of them, it is all the ego mind. But once the seer sees itself in all existence, how can they be afraid? How can there be anything wrong? How can they contract? The possibility of contraction goes away. When you really sit in that knowledge, not as a shadow of that knowledge, not as a concept of that knowledge, but as your own visceral experience, then there is no fear. Of course, because of linear time and conditioning, one might forget but one must catch oneself. One must be aware of the ego mind.

The more you catch yourself, the more you can set yourself free. But don't ever think you have arrived. I've seen this happen. People think they have arrived. Don't look to arrive. There is no place to arrive to. That is chronic seeker mentality. Arrive without the thought 'I have arrived' attached to it. Without the idea attached to it. The real experience of arriving is a continual process; it is not a static experience. It is dynamic. You keep arriving and arriving and arriving. In that there is this refining and refining and refining. The ever-increasing value of awareness is arising within you, the unknown coming into the realm of the known. The Self permeates all existence and all existence permeates the Self. Self in all directions and all directions in Self.

This dynamic expansion is true knowledge, true knowledge without the ego idea. Know everything without the idea that I know everything. Know the distinction between the two; it is very important. Otherwise, it is just spiritual ego. If that happens then you must catch yourself or else someone or something else will. Your unresolved issues since childhood will catch you, your mother's voice in your head, your father's disapproval of you, your failed relationship, your insecurity when you were a fourteen-year-old kid, any traumatic experience, even the ignorant particles of people who are floating around you. Somebody or something will catch you if you do not catch yourself.

There is only the Self. Within that knowledge you will find that *vijugupsate* won't happen. You can then enjoy your idiot-ness and you can scold yourself but inside you know it doesn't matter. It's okay. Only when you realize that nothing matters can you be the one for whom everything matters. Otherwise you are nothing but a cartoon, a caricature of a human being. Only those who have reached the very depth of the emptiness of all phenomena, who are moving in that direction, can really, truly care.

When one sees one's existence, it is very powerful. To correct one's intellect is of the greatest power. When your intellect is going all crazy, don't try to understand the problem. Don't try to understand how to deal with this person or that situation, realize it means nothing. You don't exist, the person doesn't exist, your interactions don't exist. You are nothing more than a cosmic sneeze and nobody cares how two sneezes interact with each other. Realize that. Then as you correct your intellect, you find you have become all caught up in something that doesn't need so much attention. Gain clarity. Contemplate. What is contemplation? It is not you just sitting and thinking. Start clearing. In contemplation what we do is create a clearing, a frame, a context. Then we set our mind free, free to roam within that field. Contemplation is important, it's a very good practice. Be relaxed for thirty minutes and contemplate. Try it.

यस्मिन्सर्वाणि भूतान्यात्मैवाभूद्विजानतः ।
तत्र को मोहः कः शोक एकत्वमनुपश्यतः   ॥७॥

7. *Yasmin sarvani bhutany atmaivabhud vijanatah tatra ko mohah kah sokah ekatvam anupasyatah.*

When the seer starts to see their own Self, their own Cosmic Self, when one starts to experience one's own Cosmic Self, one's own timeless nature, then how can one crave anything? How can there be attachment or aversion? How can one exist in delusion? How can one experience any suffering?

You see, for there to be suffering, this bag of skin has to be attached to identity. Outside this bag of skin suffering cannot exist. All suffering one has, all problems one thinks one has, all disturbances one feels one has, are only from the point of view of an awareness which is enclosed in this bag of skin. No matter how sophisticated its vocabulary, how educated its table manners, as long as the awareness is fundamentally still logged in as this isolated bag of skin, it suffers. All the bags of skin, isolated bags of awareness, which are suffering are creating the suffering. Then we find these isolated bags of awareness creating suffering for other isolated bags of awareness.

Feeling moved deeply by something is a very different thing from just making a lot of noise about stuff. People who cultivate this melodramatic attachment to suffering cannot impact the earth in a positive manner, in any shape or form. What this mantra is saying here is, how can the one who sees their own cosmic nature suffer? And the one who doesn't suffer cannot create suffering. Only the one who has transcended suffering can bring peace, can bring compassion. All suffering exists within the isolated point of awareness. Outside that isolated point, there is no suffering so therefore one cannot suffer. As one ceases to suffer, one is filled with compassion, with a great love for all those who are suffering.

In life, pain is inevitable. Don't confuse pain and suffering. Pain is growing; growth is pain. Suffering is totally self-created. It is a product of ignorance. Suffering is a clear sign of your ignorance. So, when you feel in pain, instead of looking for someone to blame, to find fault with, transcend wherever you are. Go where you are not yet. Only when you can do that can you really make any impact, can you really help, really serve. Then one's presence uplifts all sentient beings.

One who believes they are suffering secretly enjoys it when other people suffer. They secretly hope for somebody else to suffer, then they secretly feel better about themselves. It even has a name, this feeling, *schadenfreude*, to be happy when someone else fails; people secretly hoping for other people to suffer. And when it happens, these people feel slightly better because misery seeks company. The miserable seek out more of their own kind to confirm the misery. Ecstasy doesn't seek company, it shares its joy. It naturally shares it and because it is naturally sharing it, it always has company. It's the nature of nature.

Nobody should suffer. May all sentient beings transcend suffering. When you are suffering, the only thing you are interested in is that you stop suffering. That is one's primary objective: to stop suffering. The way out of that suffering is not by blaming others. The way out of that suffering is to wake up to one's truth. The mantra is saying when the seer can see, when the knower starts to know that there is only the knower, how can there be any pain, any suffering? How can there be any grief left? For there to be this grief, there has to be an objective in this seemingly isolated reality; somebody else is doing something to you. When the knower realizes that there is only the knower, then one can understand that this 'life' is only a film, a show, a melodrama. Then the fear of the movie ending stops, the fear of what might happen next ends. It is replaced by enthusiasm, by excitement. There is no fear of what might be. Just like watching a movie, in order to enjoy it you have to enter the world of the movie. You get invested in it, your heart rate goes up, you don't want anything to happen to the hero. Then you have to remind yourself, this is just a movie, nothing is actually happening to that person, it's not real.

Like in a movie, in life you have to catch yourself, remind yourself, this is not real. And in that you find enjoyment. You enjoy the anticipation. You enjoy the suspense. You enjoy the drama. Once you realize it is not true, once the knower knows the truth behind all the phenomena, truly knows, truly starts to see it not merely as a concept but really begins to know it, then the knower sees the truth of their own consciousness playing as individuality. Then there is no fear, no grief is left. It is all held in ecstasy, even the pain. That's why we say at the end of pain there is love. Every phenomenon, all experience, is held within love.

The knower, the known and the experience of knowing is only the Self. And as the Self wakes up to this value, this truth, then they are no longer caught up in the drama. Instead they can enjoy it, can play with it. That's why we say, be in the world but not of it. That is not to say there is no pain. Yes, there is still pain. As you illuminate, as you move deeper and deeper within the realm of your own consciousness, it does not mean that you become pain free. No, pain is there. But now this pain is held in deep love. Challenges are held in deep love. Tears are held in the chalice of ecstasy. Because without pain there would be no ecstasy. The pain is only an expression of ecstasy, an expression of love. It's what makes the 'movie' really worth experiencing. When somebody you admire, somebody you have a connection to, drops their body no matter how awake you are, if you do not experience pain you're inhuman, you are not awake. Pain is an extremely relevant experience. But this pain is free of grief. This pain is only a part of love. This pain is an expression of the leela. We are not afraid of pain.

The Self is not the story. If you really observe the Self, then you know the distinction. The Self is before the story. It is the Self that is weaving the story. It is not the story weaving the Self. Most people think that the story is weaving the Self. That is the ego state. What is the ego state? That the story is weaving me. When you really observe, you find you cannot locate that suffering. For there to be suffering there has to be a weaving of a narrative. And then the individualized self has to be at the end of that narrative. But when you really observe, you cannot find that so-called suffering independent of the narrative, of the story you are telling. If you take away the narrative, you don't find suffering. You find only an experience. For there to be suffering, there has to be a narrative attached to that experience. For that suffering to continue, as it does for most people, the self has to be at the end of that narrative, unobserved. Then what is observed is only the narrative.

When you talk to people, what they tell you is their story. They are only observing the story, the narrative, which they think they have nothing to do with. They don't realize it is only them creating the story. The knower, the known and the process of knowing, is nothing but the Self. When the Self remains unobserved, the story continues. But when you really observe, you will not find the suffering, I guarantee this. All you will find is the narrative, the story. If you really don't attach to any of it, any made-up meaning, you will find that what you are left with is an experience in the depth of your own being. And if the experiencer is the experience, then what you make of it is all within the domain of your own authority. What you make of that experience is your choice, no one else's. The knower, the known and the process of knowing. This whole culture of keeping the narrative intact, this obsession with suffering, it's like an addiction. It's really fashionable to suffer; like it's trendy to remain a victim.

Suffering yourself is not how you are going to change the world. The sufferer can only change the world when they are not in the state of suffering. As long as you are in the narrative of suffering you are an angry person and angry people do not make the world a better place. When you are in anger, you are in violence within yourself. Your life in that moment does not get better, so how can you make anybody else's life better? Only once you have let go of the suffering can you change the world for the better. When you find yourself weaving this narrative, this state of suffering, you must observe yourself. You will find, okay this happened, that happened, but where is the Self then? When you really look, the only place you can locate that suffering is in the story. If there is no story, you won't find the suffering.

People are obsessed with their interpretation about what happens because they can only find themselves, they only know themselves, within that narrative. They do not know who they are beyond the narrative they have woven. For them to let go of that narrative, no matter how false, how violent, how regressive it is, is so difficult because they can only locate the ego within that narrative. Their consciousness is obsessed with the ego state, so they have to maintain this violent narrative. Culturally and individually. That's what we find humanity doing, maintaining narratives culturally and individually which are regressive, which are violent, because there is a collective state still within the grip of the ego mind.

If you don't attach to any of it, then what you are left with is just the Self and the experience of the Self. The experiencer is the experience. The observer is the observed. Then you are free. Then you are in ecstasy. Dancing. When the knower knows all beings as their own Self, how can there be grief? This is the bodhisattva nature. Awakened. The ecstatic Self. Wonderful. There's some powerful stuff in these Upanishads.

स पर्यगाच्छुक्रमकायमव्रणमस्नाविरँ शुद्धमपापविद्धम् ।
कविर्मनीषी परिभूः स्वयम्भूर्याथातथ्यतोऽर्थान्
व्यदधाच्छाश्वतीभ्यः समाभ्यः ॥८॥

8. *Sa paryagac chukram, akayam, avranam, asnaviram, suddham, apapaviddham kavir manisi, paribhuh, svayambhuh, yathatathyato'rthan. Vyadadhac chasvatibhyas samabhyah.*

Sa paryagāc, the Self is self-illuminated. This mantra is expressing certain qualities of the Supreme Being, Brahman, the Supreme Self, which is all-pervading. As we've already established, the Supreme Being is motionlessness, changeless. For there to be motion, there has to be change. For there to be movement, one has to be present at one location and absent at the other. And the interval that happens in this change of location is what we call time. So, as I explained, time is ultimately a way of measuring change. The Supreme Being by its essential nature is timeless. All-pervading. Omniscient. Self-illuminated. It's quite brilliant. *Akāyam*, without any muscle; it is without any muscular structure. It's not saying it doesn't have form, but this form is not of the five-sensory kind, not how we with our five senses experience form. Since it is without any muscle, the Supreme Being can take on any form. What it is talking about here is this quality of the Self which is self-illuminated, self-aware.

The lower mind is always aware of something external to itself. When we say awareness, it is an awareness which is directed toward something other. Whether it is a thought, a flower, a person, a pizza, whatever it is, it is an external awareness. What we are talking about here is that the Supreme Being is self-aware. This unique quality of awareness is not hinged on anything externally. For there is nothing which is external to that. Since there is nothing that is external to that, all awareness is pointing to itself only. So the Supreme Being is self-aware, self-referral. One can verify this right now, because right now one is experiencing this moment, and one is aware of this experience, and then one is aware that one is aware of the experience. There is an experience occurring and the experiencer is the experience. The experience and the experiencer are inseparable. The experiencer in this very moment is aware of the experience occurring and there is also a subtler awareness that one is aware of the awareness of the experience.

Awareness is fundamental to the nature of reality and the Supreme Being; by its essential nature it is self-aware. This awareness includes all dimensions. What we call ego is an isolated point of awareness. Awareness is there but it is isolated so this awareness is extremely limited in its scope. This is not self-referral. It can only be aware with external stimuli. All its awareness is object-driven, narrative-driven, thought-driven. As the infinite Supreme Being expressing itself in point values of itself, it is unaware within its point value. In its infinite value it is forever and ever aware.

Now that is quite a brilliant thing because if that same infinite value is fully aware, yet in its point value it is not aware, that naturally must mean that self-awareness is hiding within that point value. So we can find it. We can verify this from our own experience. That's why we practice. When we practice, we find we can access the great depth of silence within ourselves and then a different quality of awareness starts to become available to us. Supreme knowledge. We find that that which was once not aware, that being who was once not aware, starts to become aware. So, it must mean that that self-awareness was hiding in the point value which was once not aware.

When one goes deep within to that stillness, one finds there is a movement occurring. This movement is a movement of consciousness within itself. As I said in the 5th mantra, it moves and yet it moves not. This consciousness is self-aware and this awareness has no origin. At the very fundamental value of reality is a conscious, aware field. When we transcend thought and dive deeper within ourselves, we find our awareness expands. That is why the yogis call it sat chit ananda. As we go deeper within, we access this dimension which is changeless and this changeless dimension refines and expands our awareness. Essentially the nature of this field has to be aware. For our physiology, our individuality, is arising from this, the Supreme Being. Since this individuality is arising from this unified field, the Supreme Being has to also be self-aware. Right now, we can verify this. We are aware that we are having an experience and we are aware that we are aware of having that experience. That gives us a great edge, a great advantage, that we are aware that we are aware of the experience.

The nature of the Supreme Being is to be self-aware and also self-illuminated. *Paryagāc chukram*, all-pervading luminosity. Is that not magnificent? The nature of the Supreme Being is all-pervading luminosity. When we look at the universe, we find it is filled with light. The fundamental nature of the universe is light; that is why it is visible. And we find within our own practice, say in our morning meditation when we are using the mantra, we refine our awareness of the mantra and then there comes a time when the mantra just dominates, everything starts to cancel out and it starts to create this charm. When you start to follow this charm, the mantra drops and what you find instead is a faint glow. You discover a subtle glow of consciousness, which in all traditions has been called the light of the Divine. In all the different traditions, Abrahamic traditions, native traditions, wherever you go, you find this 'light'. The light is the constant. Even in Einstein's Theory of Relativity, he used the speed of light as the constant.

Light is the fundamental fabric of reality and the nature of the Supreme Being is to be self-luminous, meaning light without a source. Any source of light, by its very nature, is burning itself out while in the process of giving light, of illuminating. Hence it is bound by time and moving toward darkness. If we light a candle, that candle is burning itself into darkness as it creates light. In the realm of the five senses, anything that is a source of light: light bulbs, fluorescent bulbs, LED lights, they can only stay illuminated for a certain duration. But this light, the light of the Supreme Being, does not come from a source. It is not something which is burning itself out to give light. This light is very much woven into the field of great silence, embedded in it. It has this glow. This glow of consciousness. The light of the Divine has no source. It will never burn itself out.

The Supreme Being is without source; nothing is causing this shapeless, formless being to exist. In this very moment, the shapeless, formless being is expressing itself in shape and form but the shapeless and formless has no source. Only the shape and form have a source. That which is formless, shapeless, all-pervading, permeating everything everywhere, has no source. The Supreme Self is without source. Why is it without source? Because it is subtler than time. That which is subtler than time has to exist beyond time. Only something which exists within time has a beginning and an end. Something which does not exist within time cannot have a beginning and an end. The formless has no beginning, no end.

So, the Supreme Being in its essential nature, Hanuman in his essential nature, Shiva in his essential nature, Buddha in his essential nature, you in your essential nature, are all shapeless, formless, all-pervading, self-luminous, self-referral. If you are really consistently practicing, you will find your consciousness becomes more and more self-referral. What is self-referral? Awareness that you are not dependent on external stimuli to function in an optimal manner. A weak being will always need external stimuli, external validation, to function well. But the yogi finds that their joy becomes self-referral. It comes from within. Joy now freed from external stimuli with a greater and greater value of sat chit ananda.

Kavir, wise one. Unpierced by any evil. There is no sin there. At this dimension there is no sin; no concept of sin, of wrong doing. At this level of being, there is no right or wrong. You and totality are one. If you are one with totality, that totality includes everybody. When we refine our nervous system, our awareness, then our capacity to understand others naturally increases, our intuitive awareness increases. We find this when we are with great teachers, great Masters. My Guru always knew what I was thinking but he did not show it. He just acted innocently. When the Supreme Being knows something, it has an innocent behavior. That is mastery. We find that the true Master expresses in a very innocent manner. An expression which is backed by thought is not mastery; thoughtlessness is the greatest expression of mastery. Innocent expression of supreme behavior is a masterful quality.

This is such a very powerful mantra. Self is existing through Self only. It has no beginning; it has no end. Pure being, this is subtler than time. At that level we are timeless, untouched by evil. There is no evil there. No wrong doing. No shame. No guilt. But one must not fool oneself. When one is in the relative field of reality, then at that level of consciousness, there is right and wrong. When we go to subtler levels, we find different laws become available to us. We are not bound by the same rights and wrongs. We find that in society the choice between right and wrong is very narrow. But when one can come out of that, one can play with it in a relevant manner, a subtler dimension with no judgment, no opinion. Only unconditional love is there.

As you access that level of unconditional love within yourself, you find there is no right or wrong. You access the dimension of no judgment. For there to be right and wrong, one has to be living at a level where there is constant judgment. Hence, judgment can only exist in the absence of love. Where there is true love, there cannot be judgment because judgment which is destructive, which destroys us, can only exist in the absence of love. In the presence of unconditional love, there is no judgment, no evil.

The Supreme Self is untouched by time, untouched by any right or wrong, self-illuminated, self-referral, self-existing, without source. The supreme light of all lives. This Supreme Being is at the base of all reality, is at the base of all form. This Supreme Being allots different roles to different aspects of nature, that creative impulse of natural intelligence. There is a flow of energy. This flow of energy gives rise to creation, to sustenance, to destruction. For the flow keeps flowing. Creation, sustenance, destruction. We don't have to do anything, the form does nothing. The form just has to wait to become formless. Any form given enough time will eventually return to the formless. Metals will rust, rocks will crumble, planets will disintegrate and universes will end. All form will be guided by the flow, for the flow gave it birth; flow is the nature of the goddess. The goddess is always flowing. Sri flows, she keeps doing that, there is no end to this play. This play has been going on forever. It will go on forever: sustaining form, dissolving form, birthing form, sustaining form, dissolving form, birthing form. Multi-dimensional, universes upon universes upon universes.

You see it all around, this is infinity, this flow. Creation. Sustenance. Destruction. Creation. Sustenance. Destruction. Creation. Sustenance. Destruction. That is constantly happening, while at the same time the Supreme Being is maintaining its Supreme Being nature. The eternal field of silence, self-luminous, rejoicing, full of bliss, ecstatic. Great ecstasy is being maintained. Great ecstasy. It's not an effort. It's just the nature of nature. This is such a very beautiful mantra.

> *svayāmbhuh, yathātathyato'rthān.*
> *Vyadadhāc chāśvatībhyas samābhyah.*

It's quite brilliant, *svayāmbhuh,* meaning self-born. It's a nice word in Sanskrit for you to know. Self-born. Logically, if you follow something back to its origins, ultimately you arrive at a cause which is causeless. But if you are only looking at a cause on the level of form, you run into a big dilemma. How can you give an eternal quality to form, to muscles, to skin, a skeleton? If you give form the attributes of limitlessness, you are bound to create a perversion. So we find the idea of god has been perverted, the limitless being limited within the narrow parameters of human thought. The problem is not in god. The problem lies in the ideas created about god. But as we start to go within our Self, we begin to find these qualities of pure luminosity, incorporeal, immaculate and omniscient. All these qualities start to become available to us within the experience of our own Self. We become self-luminous and have a greater non-local knowledge, we have a greater and greater transcendent experience and are in a self-referral state. All this comes within the purview of our experience. So just be with that. It's a very technical mantra, all this knowledge, supreme knowledge. It's really quite brilliant.

अन्धं तमः प्रविशन्ति येऽविद्यामुपासते ।
ततो भूय इव ते तमो य उ विद्यायाँ रताः   ॥९॥

9. *Andham tamah pravisanti yo vidyam upasate*
Tato bhuya iva te tamo ya u vidyayam ratah.

अन्यदेवाहुर्विद्ययाऽन्यदाहुरविद्यया ।
इति शुश्रुम धीराणां ये नस्तद्विचचक्षिरे   ॥१०॥

10. *Anyad evahur vidyaya anyad ahur avidyaya*
Iti susruma dhiranam ye nas tad vicacaksire.

In these two mantras, the distinction is being made between *vidya* and *avidya*, knowledge and ignorance. Those who move in the direction of avidya, ignorance, those who worship avidya, they roam in darkness. But those who worship vidya, knowledge, fall into even a greater darkness. Here the seer is using these terms vidya and avidya loosely to describe two distinct expressions of the unified whole. Avidya is speaking of the manifest world and vidya is speaking of the unmanifest world, the unmanifest dimension of Self. One thing is attained in the state of vidya and one thing is attained in the field of avidya. Both are relevant.

The field of form delivers us a certain experience which is very relevant. The dimension of the formless delivers us a certain experience which is extremely relevant too. So both vidya, meaning knowledge, the dimension of the formless, and avidya, egoic living, ignorance, the dimension of form, are relevant in the unified whole.

In the first usage of the terms vidya and avidya, the seer is not meaning supreme knowledge but incorrect knowledge, the shadow of knowledge, the idea that 'I know'. It's not true knowledge but the false idea of knowing which is a great trap. We find this a lot in the world, humans being bound, limited, by their capacity to construct concepts for themselves. Then they limit the whole of infinity within these concepts and then they defend these concepts with incredible zeal. They fool themselves into thinking that these concepts are the truth. What they don't realize is that concepts by their essential nature are constructs within the domain of human thought. And all constructs have limitations. They are only relevant within a certain parameter. Outside of that parameter they are not relevant. If the individual is caught up in this

'I know', this false idea of knowledge, in the context of spiritual knowledge, through reading certain scriptures or books, doing a certain course, getting a certain validation, then they fall into even greater darkness.

Obviously we know that ignorance leads to suffering but false knowledge leads to even greater suffering. It is easier to teach someone who knows nothing. It's always harder when people think they know about something but they actually don't. They are the hardest people to teach. People who think they have a lot of knowledge in their mind but really have no knowledge at all. According to them, they know a lot. They are the most difficult people to teach or even to have a real, meaningful conversation with. For they are not ready to listen. They are constantly talking about, "when I did my training..." or "I read in this book..." That is a very limiting position to be in.

So, vidya, false knowledge. We have to be very aware of this and not let ourselves be caught in the cage of knowledge, the cycle of validation. We see this a lot with young, immature souls; we have to be very vigilant and not fall into this trap. People get caught up in this delusion of false knowledge. It says in these mantras, right here, that these people roam in a greater darkness. Ignorance leads to darkness but knowledge that is the wrong knowledge leads to even greater darkness. That is the trap of knowledge. Those who worship avidya fall into darkness but those who worship vidya fall into greater darkness. There has to be constant refinement. We should never reach a conclusion to our refinement, never say, "Oh, I'm refined now, I'm established in unity consciousness." If you are in unity consciousness but have the idea that you no longer need refinement, you are not in unity consciousness. If you are in unity consciousness, the thought that you are in unity consciousness will not arise. We find that the truly wise souls, the really mature souls, are profound and impactful. They are the people who can totally transform lives yet they are extremely grounded and very innocent.

So, we have to remain vigilant always to not fall into the trap of vidya, the trap of knowledge, or the trap of avidya, the trap of ignorance. The person who is in avidya does not think they are in avidya. The person who is in the state of ignorance actually believes they know a lot. But the thing is, vidya and avidya are the same. Vidya and avidya are actually only separate when one is describing them. On the level of experience, they are the same. Only with the knowledge of not knowing, the knowledge that 'I do not know', is supreme intelligence possible. Knowing you don't know shows an individual who is radically open to learning; in 'I do not know', there is possibility.

There are two dimensions to not knowing. One is a person who is extremely anxious, who is too afraid to look, who is terrified, who does not know their capacity, who does not know what is possible for them. That individual is in a state of confusion and anxiety. They do not know. The other dimension of 'I do not know' is somebody who has explored it all and exhausted all possibilities and is in a deep state of surrender and unity. That 'I do not know' is a declaration that 'I am ready for anything'. Same sentence but a totally different meaning. "What are you doing tomorrow?" "I don't know." This individual is open to anything but if the person answers, "I don't know" with anxiety, then you know nothing will happen the next day. The 'I don't know' which comes from the knowledge that 'I do not know' is what Socrates was trying to teach: the only thing I know is that I know not. That is not ignorance. Not knowing but having an idea that 'I know' is the problem. As an observer, we can see the distinction between vidya and avidya. But the moment you think that you are not the ignorant one is the moment you fall into an even greater darkness.

The other value the seer has used to describe avidya and vidya is in the context of the manifest and the unmanifest, the Supreme Self. Those who are living within the world, denying the Absolute, formless dimension of reality fall into darkness. Also, those just doing meditation, living in the cave, giving up everything and living in frustration, they too are in darkness. Those who jump onto the material reality as if this is the only reality fall into darkness. Those who fight and deny the material reality fall into an even greater darkness.

We don't have to believe in it. We can verify that anything that we perceive in the manifest dimension of reality is not so. It's just a blurring on the level of our nervous system. It's a consistent blurring. Even when you are getting into deeper states of consciousness, the blurring remains. It does not disappear. You can transcend it, but when you come to the relative field of reality, when you want to have a cup of tea say, then you have to engage in the blurring phenomenon. You cannot have a cup of tea without reality being blurred. You cannot even utter a word, without blurring. For me to speak to you, there has to be a you and there has to be a me, an I. For that to happen, there has to be a certain level of blurring which we have to accept if we want to have this human experience.

If you are here in the world, then you cannot become disinterested in the experience that is here. The skillful one exists at two levels simultaneously, in both vidya and avidya, formless and form, simultaneously. Nobody can tell whether you are enlightened or not. This whole idea that somebody else can tell whether you are enlightened is a joke. Only you can know whether you are enlightened. It's a secret. You cannot tell anybody because it has no meaning for them. If they are enlightened, then you don't need to tell them that you are enlightened. If they are not enlightened and you tell them that you are enlightened, it does them a great disservice. Now it creates a concept, a construct of what enlightenment looks like. It is the greatest secret that you cannot tell yet it's visible to those who are ready to see.

We have to live in both dimensions, in avidya and vidya, simultaneously. This manifest reality is the field of illusion but you have to treat it as if it's not while still knowing that it is. Avidya and vidya. You have to respect it; you have to honor this 'here' while also remaining in the state of cosmic identity. It is not something to tell someone else. This is something to know for yourself. A truly skilled being simultaneously exists at both levels at once. Formless and form, both are precious. The Absolute as formlessness, the Absolute as form. The Absolute as silence, the Absolute as ecstasy. The Absolute as Divine Mother and Divine Father. The Absolute as the pure field of consciousness. The Absolute as formless is not against the Absolute with form. You cannot have the Absolute as formless, the pure field of being, without having the experience of the personal Supreme Being as an individual expression. You cannot experience the ecstasy of the Divine without the Divine Mother and Divine Father. For you are here through the mother and father principle.

No matter who you are, you came from a mother and a father. Whether you are a dog or a cat or a rat, there is always the mother and father principle, Shakti and Shiva. This whole idea of isolating, creating this separation on any level, is denying the this-ness. This is that and that is this. You are this and you are that. And that is this. That is not somewhere else, it's here at different dimensions, different levels of here only. You are this and you are that and every level in between. If you are in denial of your this-ness, you are lying to yourself. It is an honoring of this. Aham Veda. Aham Brahma. Aham Prana. Aham Sharira. I am this body. When we say you are not this body, what it means is you are not just this body. You are this body right now and it will be helpful for you if you treat it as if it is part of you. Not you, but a part of you.

Those who are only obsessed with the materialistic view go into darkness. Those who are in denial of the manifest dimension go into greater darkness. It's quite brilliant. Sets the record straight. Leaves nothing in doubt. That is this and this is that. Both are true. The formless and the form. They are not separate. So when, in the yogic tradition, we say that this is an illusion, we are not saying that this has to be treated as an illusion. No, it has to be treated as reality, as something real. Back it up with your experience that it is not. Then you can exist effectively. Live effectively in this dimension, playing the role with nothing trapping you.

*Anyad evahur vidyaya anyad ahur avidyaya
Iti susruma dhiranam ye nas tad vicacaksire.*

It's quite brilliant. The formless and the form. The Para Brahman and the personal god, the goddess. In tantra we are working with the Ishtas, with the goddesses and the gods. For the formless to become relevant to you, it must arise as form. For who is the experiencer experiencing the formless? The form experiences the formless. Even when one has the deepest level of cognition, of satori, of unity consciousness, one still transmutes. Consciousness is freed from the clutches of the body, yet one is again delivered back into that body. One does not fundamentally locate oneself in the body but one is still able to locate oneself as the body.

Working with the field of form delivers us to a certain kind of knowledge and working with the formless delivers us to a certain kind of knowledge. Both are very desirable. Our experience in this and our experience in that are both very relevant. One thing is achieved through the knowledge of avidya and one thing is achieved through the knowledge of vidya. Blurring, maintaining a certain level of ignorance, is required for you to exist effectively in the world of shape and form. If there is no blurring, your nervous system fails you and is incapable of blurring, then that makes things difficult. Blurring is very desirable in the manifest dimension of reality. But the very thing which is so desirable to exist in the manifest dimension of reality also traps the perceiver within that blurred phenomenon. When trapped within that blurred phenomenon, the person is locked into avidya, the world of ignorance, locked into their own prison.

Celebration and liberation. One cannot exist without the other. The individual who is really moving in the direction of true enlightenment exists in both levels at once and achieves great fulfillment in both levels. Celebration and liberation. What is achieved in dealing with form? Celebration. And what is achieved by knowing the formless? Liberation. One cannot be liberated without knowing the formless dimension of reality. But one cannot celebrate it without knowing the dimension of form. You can kick a soccer ball only in the form-full reality and there is a great pleasure in kicking a soccer ball but without the backing of the formless you cannot celebrate it. It will only last a very short time. And without the knowledge of form, and effectively existing in the dimension of form, the formless will not be grounded. It will remain as an abstract idea, the form-full fooling itself. Then it escapes into the concept of the formless while building up stress which will eventually explode.

We are living in an interesting time, in the time of a lot of words. So the illusion of knowledge is very strong. You find a lot of people stuck in the illusion of knowledge. They think they know but they do not know at all. Let's not fool ourselves. Formless and form-full both deliver us to something very profound.

विद्यां चाविद्यां च यस्तद्वेदोभयँ सह ।
अविद्यया मृत्युं तीर्त्वा विद्ययाऽमृतमश्नुते   ॥११॥

11. *Vidyam cavidyam ca yas tad vedobhayam saha avidyaya mrtyum tirtva vidyayamrtam asnute.*

Ayamrtam asnute, ayamrtam like ayamrtat in the Mahamrityunjaya mantra. *Ayamrtam* meaning immortality.

In this mantra, the seer is talking about the two values, *vidyam cavidyam*. Wow. *Vidyam* being what? The supreme knowledge. So, the knower, the known and the process of knowing are all expressions of consciousness and here the seer is talking about vidya and avidya, the two expressions of the relative experience of life together. Known together and not just in isolation. So, avidya is the manifest dimension of reality, the singularity taking shape and form from plurality. That form and shape ultimately being empty. All phenomena that arise within the relative field of reality are expressions of emptiness. As we've said, it requires a certain level of blurring which takes place in the relative field of experience. All that we experience requires a certain level of blurring of consciousness. Even the experience of time ultimately is a blurring phenomenon. For when we go into the subatomic realm, we do not find time the way we experience it here.

Time as we understand it, as it is experienced by this particular nervous system, requires a certain level of ignorance. All the experiences that we have in this relative field of reality require a certain level of ignorance. If there is no ignorance, there is no experience of plurality and so no individuality can be experienced. For if you are not an individual, you are not able to have pasta. If you want to be able to enjoy the pasta, you have to maintain a certain level of ignorance. If you want to stay relevant within the domain of the relative field of reality, a certain level of limitation has to be maintained. It's all just different states of consciousness.

The seer is saying that the Supreme Being is the one who realizes simultaneously both avidya and vidya, vidya being the absolute and avidya being the relative. For the relative doesn't actually exist. The relative is only a phenomenon which arises within the domain of the Absolute. What ultimately exists is the Absolute. The waves are a phenomenon of the

Absolute; ignorance is this blurring that arises in the relative field of phenomenal life where things appear not the way they actually are.

We can easily verify this, just look around. Look at colors, red, yellow, green. Things really look like they are that color to us. We observe and life seems to actually have objective reality. On the fundamental level, for most people, the experience is "I am this body, that's all I am." Even though one might have concepts of being a soul, the fundamental experience is that 'I' am this body. When we sit alone with our thoughts, they are dominated by the idea that we are this body, fundamentally concerned only about the narrative of this body. Even the idea of a soul is within the context of the body. When we say 'my soul', it's really the personality saying it. But if the soul is beyond the personality then how can it be 'mine'? The soul is not a personality. It has a closer value to the Absolute.

This relative field of experience maintains its consistent power over consciousness. Even though we intellectually know that it is empty, it is so consistent in its solid expression that it keeps us fooled enough to play the life game. That's what we do, play at life. That's what we are doing right now. In our challenges, in our melodrama, in our angst to become somebody, to be known for something, whatever it is we're doing, it's all a play and it's just so much effort. But there is also an ecstasy in this reality. But for this to be maintained there has to be a certain level of avidya, of blurring of consciousness. Consciousness fooling itself. It's a trick we play with ourselves; we fool ourselves. Fool ourselves into an isolated value of awareness. Fool ourselves into seeing space as a separator, into seeing time as linear. Beginning, sustenance and end. Beginning, sustenance and end.

As I said in *This Is That*, my interpretation of Patanjali's Yoga Sutras, Padas 1 and 2, the purpose of the manifest dimension of reality is twofold: celebration and liberation of the seer. Avidya is the manifest reality; for that to be celebrated there has to be a certain level of ignorance. So here the seer is saying, the true master, the true seer, knows both avidya and vidya simultaneously. The absolute dimension and the relative expression. Through this knowledge one becomes immortal; one gains immortality within time.

For there to be the idea of immortality there has to be time and timelessness both together.

If there is no time, the concept of immortality cannot arise, for there is no death. If there is immortality, it means there must first be mortality. Death is primary. Something must be dying first for there to be the idea of immortality. Only once we observe that there is death, can we discover the deathless. If there is no death, then you cannot discover the deathless. For you cannot discover light if you have no experience of darkness. If you have no experience of silence, you cannot experience sound. Avidya and vidya must both be understood together; vidya is constant, avidya is the interruption of that constant. As the seer sees both simultaneously, they gain immortality in the realm of relative reality. When you gain immortality in the realm of relative reality, that's where you are invincible. For invincibility is only an experience in the relative field of reality. In the absolute dimension of reality, being invincible is useless. You don't need to be invincible there. Who will you play at being invincible with?

It really is such a brilliant mantra. The seer is saying, by realizing, by cognizing, both values of self: avidya, self within the domain of the relative field of reality, and vidya, Self in the absolute domain, one can gain immortality. Deathless does not mean that one does not die. Deathless means one dies in the physical sense of the body but remains in spite of death. Only then is there deathlessness. But deathlessness cannot exist without death. Death is the essential ingredient in deathlessness. For there to be eggless cake, there has to be cake which has eggs. Why? Because all cakes have eggs. If all cakes since the beginning of baking were without eggs, then there would be no eggless cake. Then there would be cake 'with egg'. If all cakes were vegan, then you would have to announce the non-vegan cake. Non-vegan cake made especially for the vegan intolerant.

So, how can one realize one's deathless nature without dying? It is not possible. For one to realize one's deathless nature, one has to die. There has to be the experience of death and for death to be there, there has to be time. If there is no time, there is no death. Time, in the yogic terminology, is the biggest illusion, the consistently persistent illusion. Shiva, the great destroyer of time. Kali, the Mother of Time. Time lives within her. She is before time. She gives birth to time. Death is the experience within time. If there is time, there is a beginning, there is a middle and there is an end. Only something which has a beginning, a middle and an end can actually realize the domain beyond a beginning, a middle and an end. If there is no beginning, then who will realize the domain beyond a beginning, a middle and an end? This is like the 'Ah ha!' moment for the seer, right here. You can see the excitement in the last few mantras where it builds up to this ecstasy, this exclamation. The refining of this idea and then, "Ah ha! I am that but I am this and I realize both fully. I am immortal but within the domain of time. If there is no time, I am not immortal." Because for there to be the possibility of 'I am' there has to be time. If there is no time, there is no 'I am'.

The yogi realizes both avidya and vidya simultaneously. Gaining supreme knowledge and immortality by simultaneously cognizing both dimensions of self: self within the manifest relative field of reality, within space and time, and Self that is subtler than space and time, before space and time. Simultaneous cognition, not one or the other. The field of ignorance fully realized. The field of wisdom fully realized. Avidya and vidya, simultaneously, leading to the experience of amrita, nectar. That's the last word in the mantra: *ayamrtam,* experience of supreme nectar. Where? Here. You cognize this right now, your own immortality while simultaneously cognizing your own mortality. How can you realize your immortal nature without cognizing the mortality of this physiology? As you realize the mortality of this physiology then you naturally let go, you stop holding on tight. You only hold tight if you are in denial of your mortality. For within that realization of mortality is the possibility of realizing your immortality. It is so close, death, much closer than you think.

Oh, I love this mantra, it is really beautiful. Death and deathlessness, together. Otherwise what survives is the personality. Without death, the personality survives. We have all these theories about heaven all woven by personalities. So these 'heavens' have all kinds of personality disorders roaming around in them. These personalities have created this idea of heaven and we can only enter there through a particular belief system. This death is the deathless heaven. A heaven which has not really accepted death, experienced true mortality and cognized the end of personality, and all the narrative woven into it. It is a fake heaven. It doesn't exist. It only exists in really mediocre imagination, at best. To realize one's immortality, one has to experience mortality. One has to face that. Avidya and vidya, ignorance and wisdom together, must both be realized simultaneously.

For you to experience any meaning in this life you have to realize the absolute meaninglessness of it, the total absurdity of it. Look around you, is it not absurd? All phenomena are empty. Only when we can really embrace the absolute emptiness of all phenomena, the total emptiness, can we have any sense of meaning in this life. That is what Shiva really symbolizes, this all-pervading Shunya which dances, the absolute emptiness of it. As long as we have not faced the meaninglessness of it, there will always be a crisis of meaning. There will be projection and chasing, a need to create false meanings. And then all kinds of complex ideologies to safeguard those meanings will arise. Anybody challenging those meanings will be met by others taking up arms to safeguard those meanings which the ego has created.

Humanity's tendency is to fight over absurd stuff. We don't know our stuff has no meaning.

We can see other people's stuff has no meaning but we think our stuff is very meaningful. However, what we do only has meaning when we realize how meaningless everything is. Only then will we have access to the true meaning. Otherwise, we will keep suppressing that fear of nothingness and chasing some projection. We have to embrace the emptiness. That's what Buddha talked about: the essential emptiness of all phenomena in the relative field of reality. Emptiness. This requires a very mature attitude. Only a very mature soul can have access to that. The simultaneous realization of nothingness and everything-ness, of zero and one, Shiva and Shakti. Shakti and Shiva. One cannot exist without the other. They are together, simultaneously, the expression of one.

अन्धं तम: प्रविशन्ति येऽसम्भूतिमुपासते ।
ततो भूय इव ते तमो य उ सम्भूत्याँ रता:   ॥१२॥

12. *Andham tamaha pravisanti ye' sambhutim upasate tato bhuya iva te tamo ya u sambhutyam ratah.*

Here, the seer is making a distinction between the ascending world and the descending world. We have this divisive mentality, two worldviews that we observe. The ascending worldview glorifies everything in some other place that is not here and the descending worldview is purely reductionist, the materialist worldview, the only reality being here. The seer is pointing out that both these views are foolish.

Pravisanti ye sambhutim upasate... upasate meaning what? Worshiping. Those who are stuck in these foolish ideas of worshiping the manifest and the unmanifest are blind, are in darkness. This is an expression of deep ignorance. Both these worldviews are divisive and not inclusive of each other. We are not interested in these divisive worldviews. According to the seer, those who are obsessed with worshiping, with glorifying the otherworldly there, instead of here, go into deep darkness. Likewise, those who are reductionist in their approach, seeing this reality merely as a materialistic one, denying anything beyond their own perceptive capabilities, denying anything beyond their own nervous system, are also in deep darkness. These are both ignorant views. The true being, who has realized the great value of Self into the fullness of fullness, is not stuck in this linear approach, these ascending or descending worldviews.

True beings realize the wholeness: the personal, the impersonal, the manifest and the unmanifest. For the manifest and the unmanifest are not somewhere else; the Divine is not somewhere else. There is nowhere else. There is only here. Heaven is not in another place. How could it be? For heaven to be in another place, it cannot be heaven. The only place heaven can be is here, for all that exists is here. The different locations of 'here' are mere limitations created by the position of the experiencer. The here of totality experiences itself only as here, the wholeness of here.

To the yogi it seems so obvious but interestingly it's not very obvious to most of humanity. Heaven, for a lot of religious people, is somewhere else and being here is a fall from grace. A lot of people have this tendency of shunning that which they have here, denying this life, the ecstasy of this life and this body, in favor of some unknown other place. They are waiting for nirvana; they are using this life as a waiting room. The other view some people have is that there is nothing else. There is just this that they see, that matter is the only reality. They are both in deep states of ignorance. Here the seer very eloquently explains again, that they both roam in the shadow of knowledge, that they are both ignorant, roaming in the world of darkness. These are all expressions of ignorance. It's quite beautifully put.

We are interested only in experiencing wholeness. Wholeness here and there. *Purnam adah, purnam idam*, fullness here and there. There is nothing but an expression of here. The non-local Self has no there, only here. There only exists for a localized value of self. *Purnam adah, purnam idam. Idam*, this is full. *Adah*, that is full. That includes all values but that is only this. This is that and that is this. Here and there. There is just a point. We point to 'there', to somewhere which seems far from our position but it's just a way for us to express its position;

we are pointing to 'there' but it's actually not a place. 'There' does not exist. Have you ever pointed to there? Point with your finger to there right now. It's purely pointing; pointing from the position you are occupying now. When you leave that position and move in the direction of there, where are you when you arrive? You are here. So 'there' can only be experienced when? When it becomes 'here'. 'There' is always the possibility of being 'here'. *Purnam adah, purnam idam*, for there is only fullness.

The spiritual teachings of yogis are not about escaping life, they are very pro-this-life, living this life fully. We are interested only in experiencing fullness when we are here, not when we die. We are not looking for a way out of this life, the 'kingdom of god' is not somewhere else, it is right here. You must dance in the ecstasy of life. Life is not for suffering. Why do we glorify this suffering? This whole addiction to suffering is a phenomenon of ignorance.

The human mind is captured by fulfillment, the need to be fulfilled. All human endeavor moves in the direction of fulfillment. Human evolution is not merely for survival; it's for fulfillment, that need for wholeness. *Purnam adah, purnam idam*, that is full and this is full. When we look at human beings, what are their endeavors based on? Gaining greater and greater wholeness. So here the seer is warning against these kinds of ignorant tendencies, this kind of split between the material view and spiritual view. There is no material or spiritual, descending or ascending, position. These are both half-assed points of view, both are limited, both make you suffer.

In many teachings, we find people are encouraged to believe that there is a god sitting in some other place and this is empty and only that is full. The seer says, you will roam in darkness with this kind of ideology. Others will be obsessed with just here, with this material, manifest reality and deny anything which their senses can't perceive, the limited, feeble, fragile nervous system cannot perceive. That's also a very limited viewpoint, to be unable to imagine any other realm.

An ant has a whole world, a whole other realm, that we do not participate in. A bird has a whole life that we have no clue about. We have this reductionist, scientific view and we think we know the bird. We label them, name them... it's a parrot, it's a peacock. A male peacock has a tail; a female peahen doesn't have a tail. We reduce the birds to this kind of sensory observation. But the peacock does not say, "I am a peacock." You can call a bird a peacock but it will not respond. Only if you humanize the peacock, establish a relationship with the peacock, give him a name, might he then respond to you. I have seen a Baba do this in Rajasthan. I know it is possible to train a peacock, so obviously there is an internal world there in the bird. But this reductionist view, reducing the whole of life to merely five-sensory perceptions and what can be deduced from that, is a mere intellectual observation and very limiting.

We are not interested in this split worldview. We are interested in full value living; god here, god there. Fullness of life. Life has to be experienced. There is no ascending or descending. There is no god up there. Where up there? There is no 'up there'. Just because someone once said 'up there' we look outside of ourselves. You don't find anything outside, anything 'up there'. No one has ever found anything 'up there'. But that does not mean that there is no god. You've just got the wrong address. If somebody says Anand lives in

Dehradun and you go to Dehradun and don't find him, would you say they were lying, there is no Anand? Just because you cannot locate somebody at the given address, it does not mean that they don't exist. It's just your inability to find them. It's like hide and seek, the fun of the game is when the seeker cannot find the person who is hiding. But if someone hides for too long and the seeker is looking and looking and looking in vain, then they'll get bored. Then you have to give a little clue; you have to give little clues otherwise the fun is lost.

Your own inability to find someone does not prove that they don't exist. Just because you can't find them, it doesn't mean they have disappeared and they don't exist. You just don't have the capacity to find them. This reductionist worldview, to totally deny that something you have not been able to locate doesn't exist, is a sign of ignorance. Just because you have not been able to locate it, you shut yourself off from the possibility that it may exist. This is absolute ignorance. You are looking in the wrong place. It's not in that place. It's not in the external. It's in the internal. You can verify this within your own self. You have so much juice internally. Everything that has an external value has immense richness inside: the cell, the tree, the butterfly, the bird, the rock.

Once you realize that there is such an internal richness within yourself, then when you look at a rock you see there is an internal reality to this rock too and in the ant and the tree. When you look at a bird, a monkey or a cow you can see the external, then this question arises, who are you? When this question arises, you realize you don't know anything about that bird. There is a whole world there which you can't see with your limited eyes. A whole experience of life, a full life, is right there. Birds fly off for no rhyme or reason. We don't know why one bird flies off while the other one sits, why when they are flying together, some birds are in the front and some are in the back. Why are they in the back? Are they unpopular birds? We don't know. We have to accept our ignorance in these things. There is a great power in accepting that you don't know instead of limiting it to these reductionist explanations.

The yogic path, the path of the Isha Upanishad, is one of a life of fulfillment while also realizing that here is not all there is. This, within the sensory perception of the relative reality interpreted through our nervous system, is not all that there is here. 'Here' keeps expanding; 'here' does not stop, it keeps on moving. God is not sitting somewhere else. The experience god, the Divine, the Supreme Intelligence, whatever you want to call it, is right here, just at a different level of consciousness.

New science is now beginning to acknowledge this. The Higgs boson particle for example, yogis have always known about this phenomenon. The Higgs, the field of Shakti, is the field of emptiness from where all shape and form arise. No particle has any mass. The mass of the particle comes through the interaction with the field. That is Shakti, Shiva and Shakti. Shakti is sitting there birthing shapes and forms, the dance happening, the fullness of life happening, not somewhere else, happening here. So it is very obvious that if you don't realize fulfillment here, in all values of here, then you are roaming in darkness. We are interested in the whole view. The fullness of full. We must be liberated here and we must be liberated at death. We must be in ecstasy here, this life is meant to be ecstatic, we're not interested in a life of suffering. There is this whole obsession with suffering and it's totally self-created.

The world of becoming and of being, both are to be enjoyed. The absolute field of silence and the relative field of sound. The Divine within, the Divine without. The Divine in life, the Divine in death. Ecstasy within and ecstasy without. Ecstasy in life and ecstasy in death. Bliss of life, bliss of the Divine. Being and becoming are inseparable. There will not come a time ever when time ends. Time will always be. As long as time will be, there will be expressions within time. There will never come a time when the universe ends. Maybe this expression of this universe will end. Then there will be Universe 2.0 with slight modifications; they are already existing, they are just not releasing it for everybody. Only a chosen few have access to those models of the universe. Like Garuda. Garuda is traveling all across these universes with Narayana. Only Garuda can do that, fly between universes, from one universe to another universe. A multiverse traveler.

There is an infinity of time, so the Divine has all the time. There is no shortage of time. The Divine is creating all the time in the world. Pure Brahman is creating time so there is no end of time for there is no end to Brahman, no end to Shiva. As long as there is Shiva, there will be Shakti. As long as there is Shiva and Shakti, there is unmanifest and manifest, coexisting. While the unmanifest will maintain, the manifest will express itself in multiple dimensions of life: earth planes, astral planes, causal planes, worlds upon worlds, universes upon universes, dreams within dreams.

Whether there are heavenly universes or hellish ones depends on the state of consciousness you are maintaining as you travel. You can roam in hellish states for eternity, as long as you maintain the hellish state of consciousness. Some people visit hell at least three or four times a day. Some people visit heaven. Some people even maintain the heavenly state and stay there. So we do not want to be stuck in that ascending or descending view point. We want to practice intelligent living. Dharma here first then dharma everywhere. The Sacred here. Bliss here. Otherwise where? As long as one is trying to manipulate life to get somewhere other than here, then one is never getting anywhere. One is just staying in the manipulative state.

अन्यदेवाहुः सम्भवादन्यदाहुरसम्भवात् ।
इति शुश्रुम धीराणां ये नस्तद्विचचक्षिरे ॥१३॥

13. *Anyad evahuh sambhavad anyad ahur asambhavat iti susruma dhiranam ye nas tad vicacaksire.*

In this mantra, the seer says that the realization in both values of reality, the manifest and the unmanifest, is a whole different experience. As we have said, if you are in the subtle meditative practices, you can access that unmanifest dimension of being. When you are doing a more active kriya, a whole different experience arises in you. You can go into that deep meditative state without the kundalini technique and there is a profound silence. There is great powerful bliss there but it is a very distinct bliss. When you are in the kriya, it's quite different, more feminine, more sensual in that way. When kundalini moves in you, it's like a cosmic orgasm that happens, an explosion of Shiva Shakti energy.

The seer is saying that as we express and interact in the manifest world, there is a whole different bliss value. It's bliss but it has a distinction. Like when you are sharing, there is a whole different kind of bliss that arises. When you are alone, there is a different bliss that arises. When you are alone in the forest and no one is there, there is a different experience. When you are in the silence, in the cave of your own inner world, there is a great bliss. But when you bring that value, take that deep Shakti, and you manifest it out here, you share it out here, there is a different value. Still bliss but there is a distinct quality to that bliss. Both are bliss but there is a distinction between the two.

The Divine can only evolve in the relative field of reality through its individual expressions, otherwise the Divine cannot evolve. The Divine needs us for we are the Divine. We are here to evolve. How can the Divine taste evolution? There is no way the Divine can taste evolution other than through becoming individualized within space and time. The infinite can only taste the diversity of its own nature by first becoming finite. Without becoming finite, it cannot drink from its own infinity. The Divine, the Supreme Intelligence, therefore, has to be individualized. But even the Divine has to pay collateral. Some versions have a defect in them. Even the consciousness factory goes through wear and tear. Some viruses come;

coding becomes slightly shaky. Some models require an upgrade.

So both kinds of power are experienced by the jiva, the atman, the individuality, in the manifest and the unmanifest. That is why we have a diverse practice. Different experiences arise, different refinement occurs. You have that internal dive into the shapeless, the formless, but you cannot remain just in there. You have to embody it within shape and form. If you don't embody it within shape and form, then you don't bring it down to this dimension of reality and it remains unrealized. In the Bhagavad Gita, Krishna says to Arjuna, "All these people you are afraid to kill, they are already dead." Arjuna says, "Well, if they are already dead, why do I have to take action? Why do I have to kill them?" Krishna says, "For it to become real in your own universe, Arjuna. For this to be experienced by you in your own universe, you must act. Otherwise you will remain in darkness in your own universe." We are all universes within universes within universes.

There is a great power in going into that unmanifested state but there is a great power in working with the manifest. There is a great power in working with the elements. There is a great power in working with Shakti. There is a great power in working with our physiology, in working with our breath, with our sound. But there is also a great power in working with our silence, a great power in working on correcting our intellect. There is a great ecstasy when we correct our intellect, refine it, culture it, and the soul rejoices. The Sacred rejoices in that. The soul is the Sacred, is atman, is jiva.

We must access that, for the universe is very narcissistic, very self-obsessed. Because there is nobody else, it is interested in devising different ways to experience its own nature ever more blissfully. Time brings the need for variety and we find even when we study evolution, when we study biology, that diversity is the key to growth, the key to evolution. Wherever there is diversity, there is evolution. So when we diversify within ourselves, we grow, we evolve. When we study the yogic teachings, the Vedic teachings, our techniques, our sadhana, are particularly designed to go deep inward. But we must also be active. We must create, we must share, we must uplift. This is of supreme importance. We must not just stay stranded, alone on our self-made island, and fantasize that we have realized the Absolute. In the bathroom everyone is a good singer. You have to come out. Hear yourself through other values of yourself. That is the deepest knowledge of self-love.

Distinct powers arise from the knowledge gained within the dimension of the unmanifest and from the manifest. We must realize both values. A distinct knowledge, distinct power, distinct bliss, arises. That is why we are in this form. There is an incredible bliss to being in this form. There is so much beauty in form. But form is not against formless. Form is formless. All shapes are emptiness. All emptiness is shape in potential.

We find it is natural that when we go deep into the depth of our being there is a natural expansion in our creativity and in our generosity; our capacity to uplift and make an impact increases. When you go with the Absolute in the unmanifest realm you become naturally more capable to be with the Absolute in the manifest realm. As you go deep into the very depth of your being, your capacity to be relevant in the relative field of reality increases. You find greater meaning, a greater purpose, a purposeful life. Not the fabricated meaning, which is the denial of the fundamental non-existence of any meaning, but meaning which is embracing the essential emptiness of all phenomena. It requires great maturity, great depth, available to all but few realize it. Very, very few.

सम्भूतिं च विनाशं च यस्तद्वेदोभयँ सह ।
विनाशेन मृत्युं तीर्त्वा सम्भुत्याऽमृतमश्नुते ॥ १४ ॥

14. *Sambhutim ca vinasam ca yas tad vedobhaya saha vinasena mrtyum tirtva sambhutya amrtam asnute.*

Here the seer is building on the previous mantra, the simultaneous realization of the Divine in the absolute and personal form within space and time. The experience of the Divine, what we call Ishta in the yogic tradition, is ultimately one's own deepest, essential Self.

As we go deeper within the realm of our own experience, when we have a moment of grace, or when we have that experience of super-cognition and spirit moves through us in a profound manner, it primarily first arises in the field of our consciousness as something greater than us. It does not arise saying, "Oh, this is me." When you really see that moment of grace, it always arises as something greater than you. You are naturally pulled to bow. You are moved to tears. Love is there. You feel a presence. Not the presence, a presence. This is a personal experience of the Divine. A very personal experience of the Divine. A very deeply intimate experience. This you cannot share with anybody. It's your personal experience of the Divine.

That is where the teachings of Ishta in the Yog- Vedantic tradition arose. Not from this idea of a creator of it all. This talking to deities comes from that tradition, not like the Greek idea of a warring community of superhumans, a kind of Marvel world, superheroes who are just fighting with each other. This cognition of the deities really is a personal experience of the yogi. When the Divine arises within the domain of one's own consciousness, it arises as a personalized expression. It arises as a being with a very human-like quality.

So this is a human 'god'. Whether it looks superhuman or not, it has human elements: love, compassion, eyes, breasts, arms. It arises as a personal experience of the Divine Mother or the Divine Father within space-time which is ultimately the expression of Para Brahman. It is only the ignorant who have this debate over the impersonal and personal. Only those who are ignorant of the experience actually think gods and goddesses are opposite to the Divine, that singularity and plurality are opposing values, shape and shapeless, form and formless are opposing values, spirit and matter are opposing values. Those people only have concepts. The seer is warning us not to fall into these traps, not to see these as separate, as opposing values. The yogi realizes that the Divine within the personal domain is a very deep intimate experience. Within that, one becomes invincible. The Absolute Being becomes infinite, Para Brahman, Ishvara, that expression of supreme consciousness which is closest to infinity.

Closest to infinity but also within time. Anything that is within time changes in time, grows in time. And ends ultimately in time. The time cycle of a wave on the ocean is short. The time cycle of an ant is short. The time cycle of an elephant is longer, similar to a human. But the time cycle of a mountain is much, much longer. The trees will still be looking down at the bodies looking up at them with wonder many years after they are gone. Time cycles within time cycles. Anything which has a time birth has a time end. All phenomena ultimately end in time.

So in time, the personal experience of the Divine also changes for us. The Divine cannot remain the same. Sometimes the Divine arises as Lakshmi and sometimes the Divine arises as Kali. Sometimes the Divine arises as Hanuman and sometimes the Divine arises as Shiva. The Divine may arise as the light of all lights or the darkness of all darkness. We can verify all these experiences in our own meditation. Sometimes when you go into a meditation it's like you fall into it, like tumbling down, and you land in this space within yourself. But this space does not have the value of light, it has the value of darkness. There is no thought. There is no 'thing', no 'you', there is just the field of being, no experience is arising. Light is an experience; no experience is there, just the silence of darkness. The state of samadhi. Sometimes, when you are in that state light arises, a goddess arises or Kundalini arises, the Divine Mother. These are personal to us. It may be that one consistently arises, one personal to you which becomes your personal Ishta. It's different for everybody.

The Divine can arise as light or as darkness but always as a very personal experience because ultimately the Divine is the Self, Para Brahman. But in the relative experience when it does arise, the Divine is the greatest Beloved. Hence the Sufis going into ecstasy about the Beloved, Rumi singing about the Beloved, Hafiz writing about the Beloved, this incredible love affair. Ultimately, all love is directed toward self and sadly all hatred is also. But this love of the Divine that arises within us, this is an incredible love, an incredible devotion filled with awe and reverence and gratefulness. How the spirit moves us is our personal experience of the Divine and is very intimate. It is the most intimate relationship one can have in the relative field of reality. This life is all based on relationships. Some people think they are either in a relationship or they're not. They don't understand, you are in a relationship all the time. You are relating all the time. That's all you are doing in the relative field of reality. You cannot not relate. Relating is what we all do.

In this relative field of reality, the most precious, most intimate experience of relating is that experience of the infinite arising within one's consciousness; the Divine arising as a personalized expression, the Supreme Being. The localized value of the non-local Self is an incredible thing. It has an experience of a supreme, higher consciousness, the non-local value arising as the local value. This is what we call Ishta. Gods. Goddesses. They are all an expression within space-time, the singularity manifesting in plurality, and that experience is what the seer is talking about. For the yogi, the impersonal and personal form of the Divine are both realized because if only the personal form of the Divine is there, then there is conflict: my god versus your god. This is incomplete samadhi, incomplete realization, and leads to conflict. Impersonal without the personal. All dry, no juice. No ecstasy. No bliss. No dance. Flatlining. For wherever there is individuality, only the individual experience can arise, your personal god, at whose feet you bow and surrender. The Absolute Divine, maintaining the whole.

There is a great juice in having a conversation with your form of the Divine. There is an ecstasy to having this personal relationship with the Divine but you must realize it is personal. It is not universal. Not everybody will have the same experience, the same understanding of that particular expression. And that is not at the expense of the Divine in the shapeless, the formless, the absolute pure consciousness, sat chit ananda. That is the Divine and this is the Divine. The impersonal form of the Divine: the formless, shapeless, attribute-less. The personal form of the Divine: with form, with shape, with attribute. Ultimately, all are expressions of Self just at different levels of elegance, different levels of expansion.

Devotion and wisdom are only separate from each other in ignorance. As the ignorance becomes less and less what arises is wisdom and love, wisdom and devotion. They have the same fragrance. They are from the same value. They cannot exist without each other. Great humility and great knowledge, a strong spine and a soft heart. There is a god and there is a goddess, there are gods and there are goddesses, there is no Divine and I am the Divine. All are true. For one to be true, the other doesn't have to be false. That is ignorance, limited knowledge. This idea that for one to be right the other has to be wrong shows the limit of one's knowledge, very low, narrow knowledge. So, this personal experience of the Divine is within the realm of time, within the field of avidya, and is neither lower nor higher. As we refine our understanding, the personal form of the Divine and impersonal form of the Divine dance together.

When we relate in the relative field of reality which is in the domain of space and time, we have our personal forms of the Divine. In the absolute state of silence in one's being, the infinite ocean of consciousness, is Para Brahman, the impersonal form of the Divine. Within space-time is the localized expression of that infinite consciousness, the infinite ocean taking shape and form within the field of one's own consciousness. Personal and impersonal both have to be realized. And that's where we gain true ecstasy of being, from this deep recognition of both.

With your personal form of the Divine, you are never alone. You always have somebody really great to talk to. They know all the answers to everything and are not afraid to kick your ass too. Even when you grow old, you remain like a child when at the feet of the great Divine, while maintaining your absolute, infinite nature, you as pure consciousness. There is a great ecstasy in experiencing love like that. What is a life which has not experienced love like that? It's a waste of a life. Life without love is no life. And a love which is not experienced at its highest value is no love. The highest value of love is this love, otherwise it's a great promise lost, a great opportunity lost. This personalized expression of the Divine, this love which sets you free, is love that has no opposite. And anybody who comes in touch with you gets touched by this love and gains a little bit of their own freedom back. Otherwise the love which does not have the backing of this love is slavery. It has opposites: hate, control, blame and all the melodrama that goes with it, all the desperate neediness. "I love you so now make me happy." All very tiring. Even the love that parents have for their children can come with a guilt trip.

The personal form of the Divine is very important and nobody has to validate it. If you don't claim your own personal form of the Divine, then you remain weak. But once you do claim that personal form of the Divine, and you really go deep in your experience, you will simultaneously experience the impersonal form of the Divine. Meaning, you will gain more cosmic unity; you will become more and more part of unity consciousness. That is the impersonal form of the Divine. You are taking on the value of unity, unity consciousness. But you have to go through the heart. Without that, what's the point?

This is so beautiful. Your personal form of the Divine. Nobody needs to know about it. Nobody needs to agree with you. Nobody needs to see it. And this true, personal form of the

Divine lies within the impersonal form of the Divine; they are together. The yogi realizes both. The seer sees both and gains great wisdom and bliss, invincibility and true ecstasy, bliss and supreme knowledge. So beautiful.

हिरण्मयेन पात्रेण सत्यस्यापिहितं मुखम् ।
तत्त्वं पूषन्नपावृण सत्यधर्माय दृष्टये ॥ १५ ॥

15. *Hiranmayena patrena satyasyapihitam mukham tat tvam pusan apavrnu satyadharmaya drstaye.*

The face of truth is covered with a golden lid. This is so poetic. What the seer is saying is that the world is sunless if you stay in ignorance. The being who does not realize the value of truth in this life and stays stuck in ignorance and violence goes to the worlds which are sunless. Yet the seer is also saying what? That the face of the truth is covered by a golden lid. Not copper. Golden. 'Oh, Surya', the sun. This is now an invocation.

In the previous mantras, the seer establishes the truth, here it's wisdom and devotion. As I've said, wisdom and devotion are only separated from each other by ignorance. The truly wise is truly devoted. The truly wise is truly humble. The truly wise is truly innocent. The truly wise is deeply in love. You cannot be wise and not be in love. It cannot happen. Wisdom and love go hand in hand. In the preceding mantras, the seer has been very direct, speaking in a very powerful way, unveiling the layers. Here he goes into a total devotee state, bowing to Surya, the face of truth, hidden with a golden lid. 'Oh Surya', the seer is asking Surya, the golden light, 'remove the lid, let me witness the face of truth. Yet keep me immersed in the golden light'. That's the beauty of it. The face of truth is covered with a golden lid. The seer is asking for the golden lid to be removed, to be able to witness the truth, yet to be able to remain immersed in the golden light. This is so beautiful.

Why are we here? Why are we in this body? Because it is incredibly fun to be here. That's why you are here. If you are not having fun here, I'm really sorry for you. All the drama of your life is just that, a drama. The drama is only there because it's fun. Like Laurel and Hardy, it's funny. Or Tom and Jerry hitting each other, it's funny stuff. And if you can look at your problems as a joke, then the only things you will find there are solutions. The seers say that we are here because there is a great ecstasy in being. Just existing. Not becoming. Just in being. In that, there is ecstasy. But because the Being expresses in space and time, there is forgetfulness. The Being is overwhelmed by its own ignorance and the incredible immensity of this experience. So we get lost in our own creation and we forget the Beloved behind the scenes.

We can get so lost in this incredibly beautiful creation, in the problems and the challenges and all of that, it's just what happens. We forget that they are only there within the theater of this life. All your challenges, all your pain, your emotional melodrama are only within the theater of this life. All your fears are in this life. The face of the great Beloved is hiding behind the golden lid. For when you look at the golden lid, at that light, you cannot see what is behind it. You are so in awe of it and then you have to look away. You know from your own experience that if you look at the bright sun you have to look away after a moment. And when you look away, you still see the sun, Surya. Ultimately, that is all you are looking at, the sun. It's all the sun. This world is the sun, this body is the sun, the stone is the sun, the water is the sun, the goat is the sun, the cow is the sun, the snake is the sun. All is the sun.

Here the sun is what? It symbolizes the manifest dimension of reality. The seer is asking to be kept in the golden light and yet to also be allowed to see the great Beloved whose face it is hiding; the truth, hiding behind the golden light. We are like the deer caught in the headlights. We can't see the face of the Beloved, the face of truth. We want to see the face of truth while still remaining immersed in the golden light. It happens in certain experiences, like in our meditation. We have experiences within our self and they are mostly made up of light and sound. Whether it is the east star rising, whether it is the movement of energies, it is all light and sound ultimately in different ways.

Even when you look around you now, what you are seeing is the face of the Beloved, covered with a lid of golden light. When you look at your hand, it's golden light. When you look in the mirror and you see your face, you really think that it is you. Every day you look in the mirror, every day. And when you look, you say, "This is me." Do you realize how funny that is? "This is me, this is my nose, it's all me." Yet this 'me', which seems to be at the center of all the problems in life, is also at the center of all the bliss in life. The bliss is experienced through this 'me'. This same 'me' only suffers and creates suffering for others as long as it does not see the face of the Beloved which is behind the light.

The wise one does not leave the light. The wise one stays in the light but sees the face of the Beloved. Fully. And when one sees the face of the Beloved behind the light, then there is no darkness ever. And no fear of the darkness. Otherwise there is always a lingering fear of the darkness. A fear of not being, of being forgotten, of not being appreciated. A fear of not being needed, of not being relevant. A fear of not being desirable, of loneliness, that everybody else is having fun without you. But once you have seen the face of the Beloved behind the light, then there is no more fear of the darkness. No more fear of the other, that somebody else is out there. Have you ever entered a place where you have felt that there was somebody else there? Has it ever happened to you? And what did you do to get over that fear? You wanted to make sure there was nobody else there. When you can convince yourself that there is nobody else there, then you are not afraid. Or if there is somebody else there, you want them to be a friend. A friend is what? An extension of you. That's what a friend is. Someone you feel unity points with. When you can locate more and more unity points with someone else, then there is friendship. Unity points, that is what friendship is.

So, all our fears are ultimately based on somebody else or something else hiding in the darkness. When there is nobody else and nothing else, then there is no fear. But we must not wait to die to experience this. That is no use to us. We want this experience when we are alive for there is no life after this life. There is only life. Only life. There is no death. What a beautiful, poetic way to express such profound truth. 'The face of the Beloved is covered with a golden lid. Oh, Surya, let me see the truth. Remove the golden lid'.

When you have the deepest experience of satori, when you have inner samadhi moments, that's what happens to you. You see the light. You see the play of light. Everything has a glow, a golden light, all shapes and forms; there are no boundaries anymore. Boundaries merge and everything has this glow and yet what you see is the underlying silence, this underlying, incredible field of unity behind all the distinctions of form and shape. Everything and nothing simultaneously become available to you. Everything you have ever experienced, any emotion you have ever experienced, they all become available to you in that moment. The whole intensity of life just peaks in that moment. The end of time, end of fear. 'Oh, Surya'.

Remaining merged in the light, we live; dance the dance, sing the song, serve, uplift and stay innocent, stay like a child. Stay creative, stay real, but at the same time be aware of the field of darkness behind the light. Know that that darkness is only the Absolute, the Divine Mother. Know there is no fear anymore. An end of fear, an end of all fear. Then live a fearless life. Have you seen the fear that comes up? It comes up as doubt. It comes up as, what's next? It comes and it comes. But that moment when you are totally fearless, then just love is there. Such love and such compassion and such ecstasy. When you touch that fearless state in you, you feel immense detachment and then you want to share that. You want to share that fearless state. You want to give it out, you want to pour it out into another heart. For it is the nature of that state to share it.

पूषन्नेकर्षे यम सूर्य प्राजापत्य व्यूह रश्मीन् समूहतेजो ।
यत्ते रूपं कल्याणतमं तत्ते पश्यामि योऽसावसौ पुरुष:
सोऽहमस्मि

॥ १६ ॥

16. *Pusann ekarse yama surya prajapatya vyuha rasmin samuha tejah. Yat te rupam kalyanatamam tat te pasyami yo sav asau purusah, so'ham asmi.*

So'ham asmi, a double positive. This is so beautiful. *So'ham.* I am that, that I am. *Asmi.* Just in case you forgot by the time you got to 'that', I am that. What? That? What are you? That I am. I am that, that I am. *So'ham asmi.* I am that. Oh, the Divine can be very funny actually. This is just ecstasy, speaking of devotion, this supreme devotion. Again, that wisdom pouring out in innocence, in ecstasy, in supreme love. Both the 15th and 16th mantras are exclaiming it.

Puṣann is one of the names for Surya. Here Surya is light of consciousness, chitta prakasha, the light of consciousness, the light of the Divine, the light of being, the light of lights. 'Disperse thy rays and gather up thy burning light. I behold thy glorious form. Oh, Supreme Being who is manifest in every dimension, who is everything, gather up thy light, gather up thy burning intensity, rise up within the field of my consciousness, burn away all the vrittis and samskaras, let me see clearly. I see you. I see who you are. And as I see your incredible radiant form, I am you. I am you. I am you'. *So'ham asmi.*

Here the seer is saying a prayer. There is a realization of prayer and there is the effect of the prayer. What is the prayer? 'Let me see, let me see, let me see, Divine Mother. Please let me see now. Let me feel the heart that has supported me on all my journeys. Let me catch a glimpse of your face. Gather up all the light, let all the light of consciousness fully illuminate me, right now. Let me see the truth fully, right now. Oh, I see, I see, I see the truth right now. And as I see the truth, as I behold the glorious truth, I realize I am you'. Have you ever felt this love? Where you see something or somebody, maybe the evening sun, maybe the morning sun, maybe the bird sitting innocently on a rock. The water is flowing and just sitting there in the light you are seeing more than just the form. In that moment, you are the bird. You are that rock. You are the water. 'Divine Mother, reveal to me, reveal to me'.

There is a supreme power in longing, in longing intensely. Such intense longing that the universe has no other option but to collapse. Infinity has no other option but to collapse in front of you right here and right now. The Divine has no other option; the Supreme Self has no other option. There is such power in that. *Mumukshutva,* that supreme longing. There is an ecstasy in that longing; it is not a dramatic longing. This is a longing not based in sadness or that anything is missing; it's an ecstatic longing. It's not a longing arising from a state of ignorance, of absence. This is the longing of ecstasy, of bliss; this is an expression of ecstasy. It's an expression of the deepest love. Not the love that is missing like in romantic songs or novels, but the experience of love. And this is what the seer is sharing with us, this supreme longing. 'Show me. Show me. Show me. Let me see'. And then in the next breath: 'I see'. So the prayer is not left unfinished and unrealized.

When you are truly in that, when you are not just singing it, when you are really in it, this is who you are. It is true. It is from the very depth of your being, not a romantic idea but from the very depth of your being. When it arises in you, you experience that prayer and it is realized

Now. Not somewhere in the future. The prayer is realized Now. Where you see and you see and you see, and in that seeing you experience unity. What is that? Yog. Unity consciousness. And the seer becomes their true nature. *So'ham asmi.* I am that, that I am.

वायुरनिलममृतमथेदं भस्मान्तँ शरीरम् ।
ओं क्रतो स्मर कृतँ स्मर क्रतो स्मर कृतँ स्मर ॥१७॥

17. *Vayur anilam amrtam athedam bhasmantam sariram aum krato smara krtam smara krato smara krtam smara.*

These are the closing mantras. This is an exclamation, a declaration, a supreme intention. 'Let my consciousness move beyond the body'. The seer is speaking to self here; correcting the intellect. 'May my consciousness expand beyond this body. May this body burn to ash'. When the seer speaks of the body burning to ash, they are saying may they be able to cognize the Self beyond the body. Then they say, 'Remember, remember. Remember what you have seen. Remember what you have done. Do not forget. May I never forget'. What are they saying? That you ultimately know who you are. This is about the act of remembrance. Self-realization, which is what? When that memory shines forth, the true knowledge shines forth, and it feels like you have remembered your own nature.

'Let my prana, my vayu, merge. Let my prana expand. Let me really establish myself in the energetic intelligence and unite my personal prana with the cosmic prana, transcending the limitations imposed upon me by the body'. The seer wants the prana to be attuned with the cosmic prana. We find that when working with our prana, the experience of the cosmic body becomes much more quickly accessible. We can really transcend body consciousness very quickly, even quicker than when in meditation. By working with the prana we can have a very visceral experience of expansion. That's why it says, 'let my prana', *vayu* here being used for prana, *nilam* meaning merge, 'let my prana merge into cosmic prana and let me experience my immortality. My mind, remember, do not forget, remember what you have known. Remember, remember, remember'.

It's a supreme intention to experience one's Cosmic Self and also an invitation to the localized mind, which is perceiving the non-local Self, to remember within its localized experience. To remember the non-local Self and not to forget the experience of the non-local Self as one experiences the Supreme Self. *Krato smara, smara* in Sanskrit means to remember. Remember these moments of deep knowledge. And it is also an invitation to the listener, to the reader, to remember what you have listened to, what you have read. Remember all this. Do not forget what you have learned. Remember what you have known, meaning not just as a memory but as an experience, as a way of being.

अग्ने नय सुपथा राये अस्मान् विश्वानि देव वयुनानि विद्वान्
युयोध्यस्मज्जुहुराणमेनो भूयिष्ठां ते नमउक्तिं विधेम ॥१८॥

18. *Agne naya supatha raye asman visvani
deva vayunani vidvan
Yuyodhyasmaj juharanam eno bhuyistham te
nama-uktim vidhema.*

This is a shanti mantra. The seer has spoken
about the formless, *Purnam adah, purnam
idam...* the mantra where this whole Upanishad
starts, and here at the end, it is referring to *Agne,*
the fire, the light of consciousness. 'O Agne, lead
me to the experience of fulfillment'. Having
spoken of the formless, here it is saying, 'let me
experience total fulfillment. Lead me to the
experience of the fulfillment that you know. I do
not know what you know'. So here Agne
becomes the Ishta, that state of deep surrender.
'Even though I have known all this and I have
spoken to you about all this', the seer declares,
'yet I don't know anything'. The seer has spoken
all about the supreme knowledge and yet at the
end declares their total innocence, they don't
know anything. They have shared the most
eloquent, most supreme knowledge but now
they don't walk out of the room as a pompous
being. They walk out of the room with

reverence, with hands closed, head bowed. That is the true seer, the true Master.

The most supreme knowledge has been given, yet in the last mantra the seer has come back to complete innocence. This is the true seer, giving us the most supreme knowledge in seventeen mantras, explaining the whole cosmology, the supreme nature of reality, in an incredibly powerful way and yet in the last mantra says, 'O Agne, may I be led to fulfillment as only you know. I surrender. Let me be fulfilled. Let me be realized as only you know. Lead me'. The seer is talking about the non-divisible reality of the whole and yet says, 'Lead me. O Agne, lead me. May I be led. Show me the way. May I be led to the experience of greater fulfillment. The experience of true abundance which only you know. I do not know what fulfillment is. I would like to be fulfilled but I do not know how. Because what I think fulfillment is might not be. May I transcend all ignorance, all attachment to ignorance'.

See the beauty of this? All the wisdom, all the supreme knowledge is being shared with us and then the seer returns to deep humility, deep innocence. 'O Agne, burn away all my avidya. Let me be led to supreme fulfillment. Lead me as only you know'. A being who lives like this is living the great life of bliss. The one who knows everything and nothing simultaneously is the wisest one. For the one who only knows everything has a problem. And the one who only knows nothing also has a problem. The wisest one knows everything and nothing, simultaneously.

So the seer says, 'I offer you myself whole. I surrender'. With all this knowledge, what does the seer say? I surrender. 'With all this supreme knowledge I have given, I surrender. I bow to thee. I bow. I surrender. Remove all ignorance. Burn it away. Burn away all ignorance. Let me be led to fulfillment which only you know. I surrender to you. I bow to you. I am the Divine and I bow to the Divine'. It's the supreme act of self-love.

So, so beautiful.

About the Cover

The Cosmic Mother, Tripura Sundari, is one of the expressions of Shakti. She is the primordial energy which permeates the entire existence, the infinite potential of being within each and every one of us.

About the Author

Born and raised in Rishikesh, Anand Mehrotra was mentored by his Guru from childhood. He went on to teach students from across the world and developed Sattva Yoga, a method through which people of all backgrounds, cultures and experiences can discover and embrace their own true nature. He then established the leading yoga teacher training school, Sattva Yoga Academy, and created Sattva Connect, the online platform for teachings and classes.

In addition to being a Master teacher, Anand set up the charitable initiatives: Kushi Foundation and Sattva Foundation. He has been featured in several documentaries including award-winning *The Highest Pass* and continues to lead transformational motorcycle journeys into the Himalayas. *Liberation* is his second book.

Stay Connected

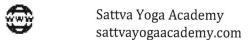

Sattva Yoga
@sattvayogaacademy

Anand Mehrotra
@theanandmehrotra

Sattva Yoga Academy
@sattvayogaacademy

Sattva Yoga Academy
sattvayogaacademy.com

SATTVA
YOGA